# You're Not the First

# Little Girl to Get a Divorce

## By: Lola Kent

# Table of Contents

*I Let the Good Times Roll* — 5

    *A. 18 and Pregnant* — 16

    *B. The Big Day* — 24

    *C. The College Years* — 29

    *D. Motherhood* — 36

    *E. Birthing Those Babies* — 46

    *F. The Beginnings of a Doctor* — 53

    *G. Medical School Had Its Flaws* — 69

    *H. Red Flags* — 82

*II When Things Went South* — 86

    *A. My Eyes Were Finally Open ... to a hooker* — 86

    *B. Alcoholics: to binge or not to binge* — 91

    *C. Christmas at Bernie's* — 95

*D. The Drink Goes On ... And On ... And On*                 *98*

*E. The Straw That Finally Broke the Camel*                 *105*

*F. Preparing To Leave Your Own Personal Hell*                 *109*

*III The Big D*                 *113*

*A.  The Beating Goes On*                 *113*

*B. DocHollywood007*                 *123*

*C. An End in Sight*                 *125*

*D: Attorneys: What You Need To Know*  *131*

*IV He Says: What It Really Means*                 *135*

*V The Aftermath*                 *142*

*A. The House That Built Me*                 *142*

*B. Consider the Consequences*                 *151*

*VI Psychological Warfare*                 *157*

*VII Let Your Inner Lioness Out*                 *166*

*VIII Empty Nesters*     *184*

    *A. My Favorite Antidepressant*     *184*

    *B. Trust and Obey*     *191*

*IX First of Manys*     *195*

*X Single and Ready to Mingle*     *208*

    *A. Getting Your Feet Wet*     *213*

    *B. She Promised Herself Better*     *223*

    *C. Him*     *229*

*XI Getting What You Want*     *233*

    *A. It's A Balancing Act*     *234*

    *B. Happily Ever After*     *250*

*XII Where Are We Now*     *260*

*XIII It Is What It Is*     *279*

# But First.....

*"Divorce isn't such a tragedy. A tragedy's staying in an unhappy marriage, teaching your children the wrong things about divorce. Nobody ever died of divorce."* *-Jennifer Weiner*

Life has all kinds of crazy, twists, turns and surprises! Getting married, having a baby, and getting divorced were three of the biggest moments of my life. Divorce is messy, and it isn't fair. Frankly, it just plain SUCKS. It's difficult to even know where to begin…that's where I come in. As I share all my shenanigans and navigate through my blunder of a marriage, I hope you find some humor and helpful bits of information along the way!

To all of my family, my parents and sisters. You are my rock, the reason for my survival. The grace, love and support each of you showed, knowingly or not, was unbelievable. I can never thank each of you enough for helping and loving us. When we needed money, when we couldn't eat, or when I needed a shoulder to cry on, you provided and supported us every step of the way. For that, I am eternally grateful.

To my beautiful children, y'all are my everything!  I would walk across fire to give you everything you need.  Watching you grow has been the greatest experience of my life.  I am so proud of each one of you and the people you have become.  I wouldn't change a thing.  We are stronger, better and wiser for the tribulations we have survived.  I always have your back, no matter what.

To the love of my life, my husband, thank you for loving us, for taking us in, supporting us, and never giving up.  You are my rock, my everything. God knew what he was doing when he gave me you, I will love you forever and always.

To my in laws, thank you for accepting us and loving us as your own, I couldn't have asked for a better family to become a part of.

To my friends, JV, JC and BC. You're support and love are endless. I couldn't ask for a better ear to listen or friend to rely on and trust, to help me through one of the hardest moments of my life. Thanks for being my people.

To all my girls at Women's, I love you and miss you all. You were my family and support, always willing to listen and help in any way possible. Stacey and Shannon, thanks for letting me have a free place to stay and a shoulder to cry on, I'll forever be grateful.

To all my SMSC girls, you were great friends, when I needed some most. You helped me move forward and learn that it was going to be okay. Ya'll were exactly what I needed, and helped me learn to love again, you introduced me to my husband, and impacted me in a way I will always remember. Thank you.

To everyone that listened, helped, edited, and read this book, thank you, thank you, thank you. Your advice and love are appreciated, your support means the world and, I am so grateful for each and every one of you. I love you all.

Last but not least, to my ex-husband, thank you for the material! I couldn't have made this stuff up had I tried; although, those years were painful, I am glad the worst is behind us!

# LET THE GOOD TIMES ROLL

They say *all* good things must come to an end; whenever one door closes, another one opens (*\*eye roll\**), whatever goes around comes around. Time heals all wounds, when life gives you lemons, get trashed with your sister... something along those lines, right?

You get the picture. Yada, yada, yada – blah, blah, blah, life is one clichéé after another. The truth is, as *painful* as it may be, sometimes life JUST sucks! Bottom line, no matter what your situation, you're probably not the first!

No matter how big or small the changes in our lives may be it's hard to not feel as though we are alone. I know, it's easy to think no one could possibly understand how you feel or what you are going through, especially when it's *too crazy* and embarrassing to even speak of; but honey, trust me, someone else has already been through it, and they survived!

They figured out how to put their BIG GIRL panties on and move forward. That, my friends, is what we are here to do. I hope you find a little comfort in my crazy, cheers!

Growing up in a small town definitely has its perks; and if you know what I'm talking about, you know it also has its pitfalls. First of all, you know everyone and *everything* – and I mean everything. In a small town, you know everything that anyone has done, thought about doing, and especially those things they shouldn't have done. You know whose aunt slept with their neighbor's cousin, whose dad's in jail, and who was seen out drinking at the local bar.... with someone else's husband. Secondly, everyone knows you -- everything you've done, thought about doing, and especially those things you shouldn't have done.

As a parent, this is exactly what makes raising children in a small town great. As a teenager; however, it sucks. Not to mention, my mom was also a teacher at the high school in town, because naturally there's only one. My mother wasn't just any teacher; she was *that* teacher the one everyone spilled his or her guts to!  (I should also mention that I have 2 sisters, one older, one younger.  If someone else didn't rat me out, one of them would - it was practically a hobby of theirs.)

My mom's most embarrassing moment (regarding me anyway) was probably my senior year.  My favorite pair of workout shorts had gone missing.  They were Mossimo – spandex – dark grey – maroon stripe going down the side – pure nostalgia.  Ladies, think back here – this was Mossimo, Mossimo BEFORE it made its Target debut.  Needless to say, I was not a happy camper. There was this girl in my gym class, she was a *Klepto*, amongst other things, and I just knew she was responsible. Several other girls had items go missing throughout the year, and she was ALWAYS the culprit. The only thing that could have been worse was if she took my Gerbaud or Pepe jeans!

Right before gym I was called into the Vice Principal's office (we had just gotten a new Vice Principal, aka, my mom's new boss). He had heard about my missing shorts, and he asked me to let him handle it, blah, blah, blah. After I left his office, it was time for gym class. When I entered the locker room, I headed straight for Klepto girl's gym bag, and can you guess what I found as soon as I unzipped it? You would be correct, my shorts.

Rage filled my body and steam was practically coming out of my ears. Her first mistake was stealing from me, her second, and largest mistake, looking me square in the eyes, and saying, *"Like I could fit in your shorts."* Say WHAT!? I saw red, and frankly, don't remember much after that. Fists were flying, or at least mine were.

The next thing I knew, the fight had been broken up; I was back in the Vice Principal's office and was now suspended for 3 days. My mother was humiliated. You should know that we kind of grew up like the Cleavers, don't get me wrong, we weren't perfect by any means – but our family hadn't ever had any *"real"* drama. I'm not even sure humiliated is a strong enough word. But hey, that wasn't the first time I had humiliated her, nor would it be the last.

Having grown up in a town of 3,000 people, I met my future ex-husband (Kevin) at the age of three. We attended the same church, same school, and often stayed with each other while our moms attended various functions. We had been great friends throughout our childhood, spending hours upon hours playing outside, digging in sand boxes, and of course staging pretend weddings. In junior high, we gave each other advice, consoling each other through multiple drama-filled relationships.

We finally began dating when I was 16, I had *never* really thought of him in that way. It was summer and we were both working at the local swimming pool, me in the office and him as a lifeguard. After spending the majority of the summer together, he finally asked me out on a date. The first clue he was no good should've been the fact he had another girlfriend when he asked me out, he had been with her for over a year. I'm not sure why I agreed, but I did. He said things were basically over between them, and that he never even liked her very much.

At first, I was a little uneasy, what kind of guy asks another girl out while he has a girlfriend?! But then, he told me he had liked me since we were kids and I was SOLD! Since childhood? Me? Really? I was practically living in a romance novel -- the boy has always loved his childhood friend, he asks her out, and they fall in love. I mean, can you say HAPPILY EVER AFTER?! I had to give it a chance, did I not?

At first, it was weird. When he kissed me at the end of the date, it felt like I was kissing my brother, or at least what I would have imagined it would be like. I don't even have a brother, so I wouldn't really know, but anyways, it was a *total* turn off. After that, we decided to remain friends.

School had started, Christmas came and went, and spring had arrived. A few short weeks before prom, Kevin approached me and suggested that we try again. He and his girlfriend hadn't worked out (she found out about our date that summer), and I felt horrible, I hated being that girl.

Kevin told me he couldn't get me off his mind, and he thought it would be better this time since we had already gotten the weirdness out of the way. He had my best friend (who was a couple years older than me, and I pretty much thought was the *coolest*) talk to me. (Obviously, hanging out with her made me the coolest too). We would get to go to prom together too, her boyfriend was best friends with Kevin! I was a sophomore and was one of the only girls my age going. It was super exciting, and definitely made the relationship seem like a real possibility. Naturally, in a small town, prom's a huge deal -- I probably would've gone with *anyone* that asked me. I mean, what high school girl is going to pass up an opportunity to dress up like a princess?

I guess you could say prom went as planned, because after that night, we pretty much couldn't get enough of each other. On one of our first dates, Kevin made us a picnic and we drove out to a place called Lover's Leap (*wink wink*). The scenery was amazing; Lover's Leap has an incredible view off a cliff, out in the middle of nowhere. Kevin had cooked fajitas. There we were, sitting out on a blanket, eating, talking, laughing…. and it began to POUR. We jumped in his car, soaking wet, and decided to go ahead and finish our picnic. We were in no rush to leave…if you catch my drift. About an hour later, we decided we should probably get going. As we started to leave, we realized we were STUCK in the mud, in the middle of nowhere! There were no cell phones, and we were going to have to figure it out, GREAT. He decided he would get out and push while I pressed on the gas. Problem was…Kevin drove a standard. I had never driven one, and I only kept making the issue worse by killing the engine... over and over and over. He, however, had a brilliant solution -- I should push on the back of the car while he pressed the gas. Nothing screams romance like being soaked and covered in mud from head to toe, am I right ladies?! Wrong. But, that's what I did. A common theme from this incident would soon emerge.

We pretty much ended up dating throughout the rest of high school. He *only* cheated on me twice, I mean what high school boy doesn't? They don't actually do that once they get married, do they? Right? No? Since they obviously don't, I naturally always took him back. I was totally that girl (*exasperated sigh*).

The first time I found out Kevin was cheating on me was after one of the coaches saw another girl wearing his letter jacket at a grocery store in the next town, about 20 miles away. Coincidence? I think not. Coach Helpful was nice enough to tell one of my best friends, and she was the one to break the good news.

I confronted him, and naturally, he denied it (shocking, I know). They were "just friends," and he had known her for a long time, they met at church camp (fitting, right?) She had been going through a rough time and had needed a friend. She supposedly "*borrowed*" Kevin's jacket one night when it was cold outside and he had simply forgotten to get it back! He even went as far as to talk her into meeting me and convincing me there was nothing going on between them (thanks for that by the way). Kevin loved me and would never hurt me. Of course I believed him! After all, we had been friends since we were little. He was just trying to be a good friend… I had done my due diligence; I even spoke to her myself, right?

The next time I caught him cheating….it was with one of our mutual friend's YOUNGER sisters. That time we broke up, and I was not having it. I had already fallen for Kevin's games once, and I wasn't doing it again. She was several years younger than me, which was embarrassing in itself. He put on a great show of acting heartbroken (Truly, he should have gone on to be an actor. No one could be as convincing or manipulative as Kevin – all he was missing was the looks). He would buy me flowers, write me poetry, and beg me to take him back. To be honest, the poetry was pretty good. He proclaimed his undying love for me in it. All I would hear from his friends was how sad he was, he wasn't eating, he cried all the time (I will say, he lost about 20 lbs. during that breakup, and he did look terrible), blah blah blah.

Then came the *real* drama, he was in a car accident, that was it; I couldn't imagine something having happened to him. When he had his accident, he came to me, crying and saying that *"his life flashed before his eyes"* and *"he just knew he loved me."* Kevin promised me that he would NEVER cheat again, because he knew that we HAD to be together! It was in that moment, I realized I loved him too and wanted to be with him.

Looking back, I realize I felt sorry for that asshole and he used the situation to manipulate me into taking him back. After all, he was my first everything...first love, first person to have sex with, basically my first real boyfriend. We would continue on, finishing high school and beginning our first year of college together. Like the young, stupid girl I was, I continued to stay in that dysfunctional relationship, lacking the ability to see what the future could hold for me. Never in my wildest dreams did I imagine we would be tied together for a lifetime.

## *18 AND PREGNANT*

It was the summer after my first year of college, and a friend and I decided to go celebrate in Mexico -- snorkeling, lounging around on the beach, parasailing. It was exactly what I needed; after all, I had my entire life in front of me. I was moving off to a larger university, finally escaping the clutches of a small town and the 'rents. I was going to be five hours away...FREEDOM!

I couldn't wait for the next chapter of my life. My best friend and I would be attending Texas Tech University, rooming together in the dorm. *Wreck 'Em Tech*! This was my last summer before moving onto bigger and better things, and I was on top of the world. I had never felt SO free, my life was finally falling into place, just as I had always planned, or so I thought.

Kevin and I started having sex that summer, so I went to the doctor to get on birth control pills before we went to Mexico. My girlfriend and I decided to go to the free clinic, Planned Parenthood. I had never had a pap smear before, so I was a little nervous. Once we arrived at the clinic, we filled out paperwork and were taken to our exam rooms (by exam rooms, I mean one room with curtains in between multiple, hard, cold beds).

Once in the exam room, I was directed to take everything off, put on this thin gown, and leave it open in the front. I got unclothed and climbed up on a tiny, cold table. As I laid there, my nerves began to kick in. My palms were sweating, and my ass cheeks were beginning to stick to the paper. *"Where is the doctor? Great, now I have to pee. No, I can wait – no I can't. Ugh. I just want to get this over with,"* I thought to myself. It felt like it was taking him an eternity.

The doctor finally entered the room….in a Hawaiian shirt with a long, curly 'fro. Seriously, he was my doctor?! He was the professional that I was going to put my goods on display for? Awesome, not what I had pictured. The exam was uncomfortable; between the cold, metal speculum and his large hands, I felt completely violated. And then it was over. I was *officially* a woman. Pap smear...check. Breast exam...check. Birth control pills...check. Priceless.

It had taken me a little while to get an appointment, and I couldn't start the first pack until after the first period. Aunt Flow never came to visit while I was in Mexico....so I chalked it up to travel and didn't really give it much thought. A week later... I STILL hadn't started!! And then the panic set in. This couldn't be *happening* to me; after all, my mom taught child development and sex education at the high school. Amusing now, not then.

The thought of what my parents would say was *sickening*. The thought of telling them still makes me cringe. I want to throw up in my mouth a little just thinking about it to this day. Yikes! I grew up in a wonderful, loving home. This wasn't supposed to happen in my family. My parents had been married over twenty years, raised three daughters, and were very supportive. Although they were often strict at times, which I found to be appalling as a teenager, they were very loving, only trying to protect us.

It had been 6 weeks since my last period. I finally sucked it up, called my big sister, and told her my period was late, she was my only option. She showed up immediately, faster I might add than living 60 miles away should have allowed her to! She had a sack full of tests in tow, just in case some were wrong…because that *totally* happens. To say my older sister is always prepared is an understatement! I took, not one or two, but FIVE pregnancy tests, desperate to not believe what I was seeing!!! All positive. Every. Single. One. We even went so far as driving to a minor emergency clinic and having them run a test. After all was said and done, I was forced to face reality and tell my parents.

I was pregnant, 18 and pregnant. How could this be? I was supposed to be starting the pill, going to Texas Tech, and rooming with my best friend. What was I going to do? Life as I knew it was over, this wasn't part of the plan. The thought of marrying Kevin had never even entered my mind, much less, having a child with him.

First, I had to tell Kevin. I mean he had an idea, but not the official results. I called him and told him we needed to talk, and he pretty much knew what that meant. I was crying, I mean how could this be happening to me? I know I've said this before, but this was NOT part of my plan. College was the plan, not a baby. My gosh, we were both still kids! How in the world were we going to handle a baby? We couldn't even take care of ourselves… I mean I still lived with my parents!

The thought of us raising a child was surreal. We talked about it for a long time, cried about it for a long time, panicked in between, and discussed every possible option. Neither of us was interested in the option of abortion… tempting as that might have been. I mean, let's get real, our entire worlds were about to come tumbling down before us. Life as we knew it was officially over. Abortion would've been the easy way out, in my opinion, and would have had the smallest effect on our lives in the long term. We could have continued with our plan and moved off to college and lived the party life, experimenting and discovering who we were. After all, this was *our* time right?  We had our entire lives before us, why should one "*mistake*" change anything?

The easy way out, however, was *not* the option we chose.  To be frank, I have never chosen that route.  If there is a more difficult path, it will *always* be the one I will choose.  I guess you could say I like a challenge…or I'm a glutton for punishment, either works.  We decided we would get married, move to Lubbock, go to college, and figure out a way to juggle a baby, school, and work.  Kevin told me he had always known we would end up together, even since we were little kids. We would make it work………together.  I have to say, he was really encouraging, constantly telling me how much he loved me and how he was going to be a great husband and father.  Kevin promised he would not be like his dad, and that he would take care of this baby and me.

Kevin actually held it together quite nicely, cool as a cucumber, while I sat there sobbing like a big, fat baby.  A part of me felt like my life was over.  I wasn't handling it nearly as well as him… and I wanted to, I did.  It was just so disappointing… I wasn't ready to be a mother.  I mean pregnancy? What's that?  That's something old people do.  Looking back, I can't help but to wonder if Kevin was happy I was pregnant.  He never appeared upset or stressed, but me, on the other hand, I cried for weeks! Typical of a man…. baby trapping me.

Now for the fun part. As long as I live, I will never forget the looks on my parents' faces when I told them I was pregnant; to say it was terrible would be an understatement.  My parents were returning from a week in San Antonio, and I told them we needed to talk…in person.  My sisters bolted to get ice cream faster than Usain Bolt ever dreamed of being. We all sat in the living room staring at each other in silence (can you say awkward?!). Finally, the tears started rolling as I began telling them of the pregnancy and our plans for the future.  "We are going to get married, raise the baby together, and both still go to college." Their response: "*Just because you have a baby together doesn't mean you have to be together*." WHOA, what? That should have been red flag #1!! (Well, maybe the cheating should have been #1, but you get the point) I was insistent on getting married and proving that I could take care of things by myself (I am the middle child, stubborn and independent). After talking for a long time, and having time to process, my parents said they would support whatever I wanted to do, as long as I still went to college and got my degree. They told me that you never know what the future holds, and that I might need to support myself one day. Girl, were they right!

## *THE BIG DAY*

The next five weeks were a whirlwind. All the planning, shopping, showers -- so much to do, so little time! And then it came…. the bachelorette party. My older sister is 5 years older than me, which meant she was in charge. My friends and I were all around the age of 18 and too young to get into most clubs, bars, or anywhere fun. So what did she do? She rented a hotel room and hired a stripper...a stripper who looked just like Fabio. I'm not even kidding, tan skin, long blonde hair, the whole nine yards.

It was a typical movie scene: Fabio knocks on the door, from what I can remember, wearing a police officer's uniform, carrying a boom box. I'm talking large, square, black boom box with speakers on both ends. And then it came… a FULL ON STRIP TEASE as he took off every piece of clothing, minus his red thong; he flipped his long blonde hair in a rhythmic motion to the music. Fabio strutted around the room, straddling each one of us while he danced, even my mother, with his sweaty body. I didn't think it would EVER end. It had to have been a world record strip tease. We were *traumatized*, thank you big sister.

The big day quickly arrived. We planned it in a rush and it came together quite nicely. That's another great thing about small towns, people really pitch in and help out when it's needed. I was already 3 months pregnant on my wedding day. We had spent the morning at the church finishing up last minute decorations and getting ready. After I finished getting my hair and makeup done, I went to put on my beautiful, white wedding dress (because why shouldn't I wear white? I wasn't the first bride in white that wasn't a virgin!). I had not tried it on since I bought it (because that would be bad luck, of course!). I slipped my pregnant body into the white gown… and crap, major problem. It didn't zip, like at all. It zipped to the small of my back and no more! What the hell? What could I do? What should I do? Red Flag #47?! Okay, in all fairness, we did get it to zip up once, but it flattened my boobs into a uni-boob pancake!!! Quite unappealing if I do say so myself! I was *flooding* out all sides of that bad boy.

Fortunately, if you remember, my mom was the child development and homemaking teacher; she is quite the seamstress. She quickly turned it into an open V, backless dress. Seriously, who does that with 30 minutes 'til ShowTime? My guess…not many. Another problem solved-- that's what my family does, we don't quit, we fix it. We don't give up; we're stubborn. We hate to be wrong, and by golly, once we make our bed we are going to lie in it (with our head held high, I might add)! I could breathe again, and I no longer had a uni-boob! The wedding was on!

 Ignoring the nagging feeling I felt in the pit of my stomach, off I went, down the aisle, knowing in my heart I was making the *biggest* mistake of my life. I cried all the way down the aisle, along with the rest of my family. I loved Kevin, truly I did (or as much as an 18-year-old is capable of). I just knew it wasn't right, my family knew it wasn't right, truthfully, everyone knew. I knew I didn't love Kevin the way a wife should love her husband, and I knew he wasn't the one…but maybe he could be? Maybe it just took a little hard work? I was terrified about being a wife and a mom on my own. Maybe it was just cold feet? I was too young. I was stuck. I was baby trapped. Pregnant. HELP!!!

The ceremony was fairly short and sweet. Kevin's grandfather, one of the sweetest men I've ever had the pleasure of knowing, performed part of the ceremony, which was followed by a nice reception at the church. I don't mean to come across as being forced into marriage either, this was my decision. It was what I said I wanted. I thought I loved him enough, and I was having HIS baby!! I just think somewhere deep inside; I always knew it wasn't right. I wanted it to be right, I really did.

We didn't have any money and couldn't afford to do much for a honeymoon, so we drove to San Antonio for the weekend. I cried the entire way there and called my mom *every* night. How pathetic is that? Who is sad about going away with their husband, and who calls their mom on their honeymoon? That's right, this girl right here! In my defense, I was an 18-year-old, scared little girl. It was time to grow up, and I was far from ready.

We had a room on the river walk in San Antonio. 18 and pregnant left us kind of limited in the fun we could have. So here we were, in a nice hotel, and I decided to put on some of the lingerie I had received at my shower. After all, I was married, and it was my honeymoon, right? Kevin was sitting out on the balcony when I decided to surprise him outside. I opened the sliding glass door, stepped outside, and closed the door behind me. All of the sudden, I realized we were locked out on the balcony. We were 30 stories high, and I was in lingerie. No cell phones, because they hadn't been invented. We were *screwed*. Did I mention I was ONLY wearing lingerie!? Luckily we were able to holler loudly enough for someone to hear us, phone the hotel lobby, and send someone to our room to let us back in.

## *THE COLLEGE YEARS*

Moving day had finally arrived, and off we headed to Lubbock. We had found a house, registered for courses, and both began the job search. We found an adorable, little 3-bedroom house. The house had a cute yard, nice neighbors, and it was in good neighborhood. That's one bonus about West Texas, cheap living. How else could 2 college kids afford a house? Lucky for us, my parents bought the house and had become our new landlords. We would pay rent to them. I was starting the nursing program and Kevin had been accepted into the engineering program, it was going to be a heavy load for both of us.

Kevin found a job as a waiter fairly easily. I, on the other hand, found it a little more challenging. Seriously, who wants to hire an 18-year-old pregnant girl? Baskin Robins even turned me down (thanks for that, by the way). I mean, maybe they did me a favor. Y'all, I get *big* when I'm pregnant, and I don't mean kind of big. I mean BIG. Maybe they were concerned about the amount of ice cream I would consume, or if my size might be a turn off to customers? Who really knows, what's important is that I *finally* found a job as a telemarketer. Yes, that's right, I said a telemarketer, literally one of the WORST, most boring jobs on the planet. It was painful, and I'm not sure if I've ever been hung up on as many times, or called more names than I was at that point in my life. It was like obstacle after obstacle of defeat, humiliation, devastation. So think of this the next time you get a call -- they don't want to call you either. The person on the other line has sunken into such a pit of desperation they are willing to do anything, and I mean anything, to put food on the table. They hate their job, they hate their life, and they are desperate for a real job. Any kindness, or just a lack of ugliness, would be greatly appreciated.

Overall, we had a great experience in Lubbock. It is such a great place, with a positive, friendly attitude. Really, I guess that's all of West Texas. The people are so nice and helpful. It's a larger city with a hometown feel. I will *never* forget our very first day at Texas Tech; it was truly unbelievable. We only had one car, and I had an appointment with my obstetrician that afternoon after class. Naturally, I took the car, leaving Kevin to ride his bike to school. Let me pause here and tell you about this bike. It was given to us by my grandfather and was about 20 years old. This bike was SO rusted and worn that we decided to spray paint that bad boy red. Go Tech! That bike was our only other form of transportation besides our beaten up, old, worn Toyota Camry. Kevin was supposed to meet me at my appointment only he was late. Cell phones weren't around at then, so I had no way of contacting him. Kevin finally arrived, angrier than a hornet's nest. I asked him what was wrong, and he began telling me about his *awful* first day.

Kevin was on his way to campus via his bicycle. On the way, the chain fell off and he was unable to repair it. Afraid he would be late, Kevin left the bicycle by a tree and walked to school. He arrived, and was walking across campus when it hit him…. he needed to go #2 in a bad way. The only problem was, Kevin was stuck in the center of campus with no idea where a bathroom was, leaving him in quite the bind. If you've seen Texas Tech, it's beautiful and spread out, with lots and lots of ground to cover. He thought he could squeeze out a fart to relieve some of the pressure, and much to his dismay, that wasn't all that came out. I'm not talking a shart here, Kevin *full-on* shit himself. FANTASTIC, truly fantastic. I still die every time I think about it. Kevin, of course, was panicked. Here he was, running late to his first day of class, and he had actually crapped his pants! Who even does that? He went to the nearest building, the English building, found a bathroom, and ditched his underwear on the bathroom floor under a piece of newspaper! Captain Commando headed to class. He can just thank his lucky stars it wasn't diarrhea. Needless to say, that wasn't the greatest day for Kevin, but looking back, I don't think it could've happened to a more deserving person.

Kevin wasn't the only one with on-campus trauma that semester. It had been hard making friends being a pregnant freshman that didn't live on campus. By this point, I was *noticeably* pregnant. I wasn't really in the same stage of life as the other thousands of people I was roaming campus with. I was taking Chemistry, and I had become friends with two girls in the band, both of which were a little on the heavy side. I was wearing leggings, the one with the stirrups on the bottom, and a sweatshirt. It was my favorite red Express sweatshirt – the red one with EXP in plaid fabric, you know the one I'm talking about! As we stood up to leave, these jackasses behind us started moo-ing. Seriously, MOO-ING, like a cow. It was *humiliating*, and I must have spent the good part my day crying. I had never been moo-ed at in my life. Who even moos at people? Rude. I was huge, a couple of months shy of delivering, and I had probably gained 45 pounds by that point. Like I mentioned earlier, I get BIG when I'm pregnant!

As for most of the college days with Kevin, all I can say is that he studied a lot!!! At a friend's house, at the library, coffee shop…. study, study, study!! Or he worked late, always picking up late shifts, always having to work overtime… Kevin was always working so hard to provide for our little family. We never had much to show for it, but I was proud of him for all he sacrificed for me… for us. I don't know if he was actually working or studying all that time…or where he really was. No, actually, looking back, I do know where he probably was! I had no reason to doubt him at the time. He supposedly worked at the Lubbock Club as a waiter, although I never actually went there to see him. It was one of those fancy restaurants at the top of some fancy building, way out of my league. I might have met one guy he supposedly worked with. I also never really met anyone he studied with. I always assumed he was being honest, after all, who would question studying or working for that matter? We were in college with tough majors, we had a baby on the way, and we were broke. Studying and working were what we should have been doing. We loved each other, and we got along well for the most part, other than the usual first-year marriage spats. We always seemed to have fun with each other. There was always lots of laughing, and we would find time to hang out with friends or get a sitter. We were good! We were finding our way…. together.

## *MOTHERHOOD*

I finally had to be induced when I was 41 weeks pregnant. I went in the night before, and was given a suppository that was supposed to cause contractions and thin my cervix. Kevin and I went by ourselves. That morning, the nurses came in, started an IV, and gave me an enema. There's a first time for everything, and for me that was the first time for BOTH. I felt a little violated, but I knew there was a lot *more* violation to come.

Kevin was very supportive throughout the entire process. The nurses started the Pitocin and the doctor came in and broke my water. Nine hours later, I was still only dilated to 3 cm and they said I would need to have a cesarean. So, after 13 hours of labor, I ended with a cesarean section. I was 18 and this was the first surgery I had really had at this point in my life, besides a tonsillectomy when I was 3. Our little girl was 9 lbs. 4 oz. and wasn't fitting out any other way. It was terrifying. I remember looking over at Kevin after the procedure while he was holding her, he was talking to her and kissing her while I was just lying there in awe. How did he know what to do? How did he know what to say to her? I think I was in shock; that was *my baby* girl. I had this image in my mind of what she would look like, but she was more beautiful than I could've imagined. I could not believe it, I was a mother, this was it, the moment I had been waiting for.

Here we were, two kids that now had a child of their own. We had done pretty well so far. We were both doing well in our classes, and I was able to take a week off before going back to school. Our family came and helped for weeks on rotation. First, his mom. This was probably not the brightest option for a new hormonal mother; I was on the verge of a mental breakdown by the time my own mother showed up. Don't get me wrong, the MIL was trying I'm sure, but I just needed my mom. By week 4, when my dad and his mom came out, we were pretty much able to take care of both of them, and our sweet little baby. We had this; this was going to work.

Kevin and I took a trip to Europe when our daughter was 10 months old. We brought her with us and backpacked all over England and France. It was so exciting. Kevin's aunt and uncle lived in England, so we were able to stay with them most of the time. After riding the train from England to France one afternoon, we realized he had left his wallet at his uncle's house. We had no money, and we had just arrived in Paris. Neither of us spoke French, and getting help from *anyone* was a challenge. We arrived in Paris on a Sunday, and most everything was closed. We were able to scrounge up enough change to cover one night's accommodation at a cheap hotel. We called my parents, and they wired us money. We reported our credit card as lost, and the company had one to us the following day. No harm, no foul. We had a blast on that trip. We saw so many amazing sites and tried so many new things. We were on an adventure, together, in this life we had created.

If I'm being honest, during those years, I thought Kevin was pretty great. I had learned to love him. I was in it for the long haul, for better or for worse. He was always telling me how much he loved me and how I was the one person he always wanted to spend his life with. Things had *really* worked out. After our daughter was born, he was extremely involved. Kevin changed diapers, fed her, helped around the house, and kept her while I was at class. In fact, when our schedules were tight, we would meet on campus with our daughter and switch off. We had one of those cute little backpacks that strapped our little girl on the front. She was so adorable! I would come out of class, and they would both be in the lobby sacked out on one of the couches. They were *beyond* cute!

When he wasn't at work or studying, Kevin would give me a chance to study or even let me go out with my girlfriends on the weekend. In fact, he encouraged me to. Although, as I am writing this, I can't help but wonder why I chose the words he let me…. She was his child too right? I was in nursing school at the time, so between school and a baby, I welcomed a night with my friends here and there. Kevin was gone in the evenings A LOT, either working or studying, so it was mostly just my baby girl and me. To pass the time, I often baked him double chocolate chip cookies…the problem was there were usually only a couple of cookies that survived my cravings by the time he got home (can you say 60-pound pregnancy weight gain? Ha!).

We had our fair share of fights and disagreements for sure, but I always considered us friends. It felt as if moving away from our family and raising a baby had made us a team. GO TEAM! Getting married at such a young age had its challenges, and it definitely made life more interesting. Working, having a baby, and going to school *wasn't easy* for either one of us. We really had to rely on each other and work together; planning became second nature.

Nursing school had taken on a life of its own. You know the saying, those that can't do, teach? That about summed it up; most of my professors were short, round, and overweight women whose only children had four legs. Have a *baby* in nursing school? No ma'am! You should really get your priorities straight. I missed one week of class when I had my daughter via cesarean. My anatomy professor actually called to check on me. My nursing professors, on the other hand, gave me a 0 for any assignments I missed the ONE week I was out.  I managed to come out with all A's that semester and life went on.

I ended up transferring from Tech's nursing program to a diploma RN program.  It had more clinical hours, the classes were smaller, and it had a higher pass rate on the Boards.  Nursing school was a lot of work: 6 am clinicals, exams in which there were two right answers and you had to choose the best one, and don't even remind me about care plans.  Care plans were the devil, and I felt like they would surely be the death of me.  If you're a nurse and you *don't* cringe at the sound of the word care plan, something is seriously wrong with you.

Kevin moved a couple hours away during our third year of college to do an internship for his degree plan.  I couldn't really just pick up and go with him; I was in nursing school after all.  Taking a semester off of nursing school puts you behind an entire year.  There is no flexibility if you want to stay on track, and they aren't going to just hold your spot for you. I was terrified to stay by myself. I had *never* lived alone; I went from living with my parents to living with my husband! He was there to snuggle with every night. It was going to be hard, luckily I had people to help.

I stayed in Lubbock with our daughter, with the help of my two best friends, and continued on towards my degree. Kevin was gone during the week, and we would see each other most weekends. My friends and I had sleepovers as often as possible. There were many nights we put my daughter to bed and stayed up laughing, sharing secrets, making Jell-O shots, you name it. It was as close to a college life as I would get. I missed my husband, but I was determined to make the best of it.

Like most girls, we decided to do a little PI work one night and check up on old Kevin, so we decided to check his email. Again, at that time, cell phones had just come out and we couldn't afford one. Email was the next best way to communicate, other than the old landline. What I read left me shocked, dismayed, and hotter than a *whore* in church.

We discovered multiple emails he had been exchanging with a girl from our hometown. Might I add, she was a total skank who had slept with pretty much every druggie or willing participant she could sink her claws in to. *Seriously?* You had to be kidding me! How pathetic could he be? She wasn't even pretty. Not only did she look like she had been *beaten* with an ugly stick, if she were an inch shorter, she would have been perfectly round. Those were my super mature thoughts at the time. We decided to do the adult thing, and immediately sent her a nasty email asking her to leave him alone. My friends and I blocked her from his email, and then I called and confronted him. Of course, according to him, they were just friends, it was all her, blah, blah, blah. Kevin loved me; correction, I was *the love* of his life. He would NEVER cheat on me…. especially with someone like that. Broken record, heard it all before. This Naïve Nancy fell for it again…. hook, line, and sinker! He was the victim, right? Of course, I also believed him when he said he only went to gentleman's clubs with his work friends because they liked it. He personally thought they were disgusting, and the women were nasty. Kevin had me, why would he want anyone else? They went ALL the time. Being forced to get a lap dance from that caliber of woman must've been really difficult, poor bastard. I guess ignorance is bliss. We see and believe what we want to. If his lips were moving, he was *lying*. I guess I was too stupid to know better.

Now let's talk about the rumors. Every time I would return to our hometown, I would hear about him cheating on me. Say what? We were *MARRIED*, with a kid. Kevin was my best friend and I was his. Why would I believe such lies? Lies, I tell you! After all, when would he have time to cheat on me? Honestly with work, school, and a new baby, I didn't have time to worry about it; or maybe I didn't want to? Even though he frequented the gentleman's clubs with his friends, I didn't see it as a big deal. After all, Kevin thought they were gross and was being forced to go. Let's get real, we were young, and he said he just liked hanging out with his friends. I'm sure that's all it was; I mean it's not like he'd cheated on me before...kidding I'm kidding. I don't know if I was too dumb to know better, or just too overwhelmed to want to know. I figured people were jealous, misinformed, whatever. How would they know? We lived over four hours away. The older I get; there are some realizations I have come to; the light bulb finally turned on. I know rumors don't just appear out of thin air; there's always some truth behind it. I've also learned that people don't just start rumors because they are "jealous." That is such an odd statement anyway. I'm pretty sure no one was jealous of my 18 and pregnant, married to a cheating loser, life.

## BIRTHING THOSE BABIES

Hallelujah, I FINALLY finished nursing school! I was 21 years old when I started working as a labor and delivery nurse in Lubbock, Texas. Although I was excited to be finished with school, I was scared to death to actually be taking care of someone. I mean, what did I know? I was a brand new RN, fresh out of school, and someone's life was going to be in my hands. Even scarier, their baby's life was going to be in my hands. Luckily, we would be orientating with an experienced preceptor for three months before being moved to the night shift, where we would then have to work alone.

There were 12 of us that started together. We would be working antepartum and labor and delivery, with the plan to move us all to the night shift. We spent hours in the classroom where we were inundated with everything we would need to know about labor and delivery. When we weren't in the classroom, we were on the floor with our preceptors, learning to start IVs and how to read a fetal monitor, along with any other appropriate actions that might need to be taken.

Learning to deliver babies was one of the most exciting and rewarding jobs I've ever had. A) There's *no such thing* as a boring delivery. No patient, family, or outcome, from losses to new additions, is the same. B) The rush you get during an emergency cesarean section, shoulder dystocia, or postpartum hemorrhage is indescribable. Things can go from calm to hairy in a matter of seconds. C) At the end of the day, you were involved in one of the most magical experiences on earth. This is one of the best and most important days of a person's life, the day they became a parent. Labor and delivery is the most rewarding job in the world. There is an expression that says once a labor and delivery nurse, always a labor and delivery nurse. Let's just say, it's said for a reason.

It was one of my first night shifts by myself, and of course I was caring for an attorney's wife. She was a *total* prima donna. You know the type I am talking about.  For the stories sake, their name was something really common, like Mr. and Mrs. John Smith.  Well, I needed to take some blood from Mrs. Smith, and I had only ever collected someone's blood out of his or her IV.  That's what we did when people came in for labor, C-section, etc., we put in an 18-gauge IV and drew their blood at the same time. This time, however, I only needed blood.  So, naturally, I used an 18-gauge needle to draw the blood, rather than one of those tiny butterfly needles that aren't as painful.  Definitely not my brightest idea. Understandably, Mrs. Smith was not happy….AT ALL.  Two nights later, I was at work when I received a phone call from Mr. Smith. He was FURIOUS about the care his wife received. He was really giving it to me, too. I was stammering, not sure how to respond, trying to be nice, and failing miserably.  Just as I was about to give the phone to my charge nurse, he announces that he is a DJ at one of the local radio stations.  Ha. Ha. Ha. The joke was on me.  My best friend, who also worked with me, had him call.  She, unknowingly, just happened to use the same last name as the patient I had cared for two nights before. I seriously almost crapped my pants...like my husband, if you will recall. That was the night shift; it was a blast. We played pranks on each other all the time.

My oldest daughter was two, I was finished with school and working, we finally had a regular income and insurance, so we decided it was time for another baby. Things were good between Kevin and I. I think my base pay starting out as an RN was $11 per hour, with shift differentials and high-risk differential, I ended up with about $19/hr. That was *A LOT* of money at the time. We finally bought a new car, and I finally got my first cell phone. We were banking, or so we thought. He only had about a year left of school, and we were quickly approaching the finish line.

After careful consideration, I decided to quit taking birth control. BOOM! Two weeks later, I was pregnant. I was excited; after all, it was planned this time, even though I thought it would take a little bit longer. Kevin was an engineering major; however, he decided during his last year of college he wanted to attend medical school. I was all for it! He was smart and a great dad. I knew he would make a great doctor, as well! Luckily, I would deliver the month before he graduated, and then we would be moving to wherever he was accepted. Working nights, pregnant with a 2 ½ year old was beyond exhausting. All I wanted was to sleep. It didn't matter how much I slept; it was *never* enough. What was really exhausting though, was listening to all my patients tell me how big I was, OR having my patients ask how many babies I was having, that was GREAT! I mean, they apparently weren't thinking about who was putting their IV in and how many tries it might take me. Kidding, I'm kidding.

I was never one of those cute, little pregnant women. I gained 55-70 pounds with each pregnancy. Did I mention I have 5 children? If I had a quarter every time someone asked me if I was having twins, or told me I was huge, I would be a very rich woman. I'm not sure why people think pregnancy gives them a free pass to say whatever the hell they want. I mean, you don't hear me saying, "Wow your ass has gotten really big!" or, "Man you sure haven't aged well. Time really isn't your friend. Have you heard of a gym, because you sure don't look like it?" NO! That would be rude. Telling someone how big she is when she's pregnant is still rude. *Ruder*, even! Women have enough to overcome throughout pregnancy. Not only is their body changing, they're nauseated, constipated, and they have an alien growing inside of them. That little person is constantly kicking them in the belly, or worse, in the crotch. They can't sleep; much less get comfortable. Being pregnant is basically like being a ticking time bomb. You're just waiting for someone to say the wrong thing so you can rip him a new one. The hormones are *raging*, and you have utterly no control over your emotions. So, think about that the next time you say something to a pregnant lady. Choose your words carefully, and I mean very carefully. You don't want to be the straw that broke the camel's back.

## THE BEGINNINGS OF A DOCTOR

Our second daughter was born in April, a month before Kevin graduated. He had been accepted to medical school at the University of Houston, so we moved to Houston shortly after. I had already worked as an RN in labor and delivery for a year, which made it fairly easy to find another job. After a weekend of house hunting, we finally found the perfect one. For future reference, I would suggest doing a little more research when trying to decide where you are going to live in a new city. Maybe get opinions from someone other than your realtor, use the internet, look up crime rates, and talk to people who have lived in a large city. Our house was in the southwest part of Houston, on a busy street, like busy enough to have 2 lanes and stop lights. It was quite the change for a girl that grew up in a small, Texas town; the only other place I had lived was

Lubbock, and that was overwhelming when we first got there! Looking back however, having all your streets in numerical and alphabetical order is pure genius. Probably not as big of a deal nowadays since you can just pull up your map on your smartphone, but it was my saving grace when learning the city of Lubbock and only having a paper map to do so.

Needless to say, Houston was quite the *culture* shock! First off, Southwest Houston has one of the highest crime rates in the city. During our 4 years in that neighborhood, the house across the street exploded, we had a drive by shooting at our house, and several neighbors were robbed. I may or may not have hit the panic button (calling 911) on the house alarm 2 or 3 times when the meter man jumped the fence. But for real, wear some identification: a vest, shirt, hat, something.

Before you start medical school they send you to a retreat. It's basically like church camp where you attend different workshops and activities. It's supposed to be a great opportunity to meet people.   During these workshops, they discussed how most marriages in medical school fail.  The stress and hours really take a toll on all relationships and few will survive.  Crazy, I thought!  Not us, we will be fine, our love is real! We had survived thus far; I figured the worst was behind us.  We had a baby at 18 and made it through college with no real problems.  Now, we had two sweet baby girls.  Plus, I'm not one of those girls who needs a lot of attention.  If Kevin was gone studying all the time, I would be *totally* cool with it.  We had been best friends since we were little. Our relationship was so much more than just a typical boy meets girl, they fall in love, and get married.  We had history.  We had been through thick and thin together already.  We always had each other's backs.  We were best friends above all.  What else could possibly get in the way?

It didn't take too long to get adjusted.  We found a preschool/daycare for both the girls.  The search was fast and furious.  The director at the daycare was a single mom whose husband had recently left her…. because he was gay. She had two small daughters and had been a stay at home mom until two months prior, when the ultimate betrayal had forced her back into the work force. She was the nicest lady, and was even willing to let us bring the girls to her house, painfully early in the mornings, and take them to daycare with her. It was a win-win for us. It turns out her husband had decided he was "*gay*" while also impregnating another woman. As bad as we may have it, it's pretty much a guarantee someone else has it worse, always. Remember, you're not the first little girl whose husband simultaneously got another woman pregnant and turned gay. Unfortunate for her, but great for us! We could not have survived without her. We had to be at work before any of the daycares opened and sometimes got off after they closed. She was our saving grace, and of course, we paid her extra, which I would like to think helped her out, too.

I got a job at Hermann Hospital. It was the weekend before my first official day on the floor, and I had completed the dreaded hospital orientation. It's the same, week-long bore-fest wherever you go. I understand certain policies and procedures have to be covered for legal reasons, but geez, there has to be a better way! Kevin had flown out of town that weekend to attend his granddad's wedding, and the girls and I stayed behind. One of my best friends from high school came in to visit, while she was there, it began raining, AND RAINING, AND RAINING. Hello, Tropical Storm Allison! It was *insane*. We were out eating Mexican food when the rain started, by the time we left and got to my house, the car (literally) floated into the drive way. News footage showed people climbing out of their attics so rescue crews could come save them. The basement of Hermann Hospital flooded during the storm, it contained not only the morgue, but all electrical control of the hospital. The hospital lost power. Patients had to be taken to surrounding hospitals all over the city. They were carried down flights of stairs while being manually ventilated. It was a CEO's worst nightmare. When I showed up to work the following day, we were divided up and sent to different hospitals to work. Overwhelming for your first official day on the job. We were placed at different hospitals for two months, and by the time I would have started back at Hermann Hospital; I had taken a job with an agency.

Agency nursing has its pros and cons. I picked the days I worked and I got paid about twice the amount; however, I never knew where I would be working, and I had no benefits. The agency would notify me the day before and send me to a hospital where I would work labor and delivery. I went to the county hospitals (Ben Taub and LBJ), Sharpstown, Cleveland, Spring Branch, Plaza, etc. When I had worked agency for a couple months, I knew the city of Houston like the back of my hand.

It was my first day at Plaza, and I went in to meet my patient with the night nurse while she gave me a report. She was in labor and said the OB would be by sometime that morning. Shortly after coming on shift, I noticed some late decelerations (these are the bad ones) on the monitor. I decided to notify the OB/GYN on call, and he said he was about 5 minutes out and would be there soon. Right about then, my patient hit her call bell. Her water had broken. I entered her room, lifted the sheet, and the bed was full of heavy, bright red blood and clots. She was abrupting (meaning her placenta had come detached from her uterus). I had not been oriented to the unit, and I didn't even know where the OR was. I frantically pushed the call bell and called for backup; they were great. Everyone came rushing into the room and we got the patient to the OR. She had a healthy baby boy and a good outcome. Welcome to agency nursing! I eventually accepted a full time position at Spring Branch. They had a weekender shift, which meant I got to work Monday-Friday, and it was 15 minutes from my house; therefore, it was perfect for me! A labor and delivery job that is only during the week, you can't beat that.

It was a small labor and delivery department, with only 2 or 3 of us on staff per shift, and you never knew what was going to walk through the door. We had a lot of patients that had no prenatal care, or they received it at the county hospital, but showed up at our hospital to deliver. There was even a physician that gave them prenatal care, set up right outside our hospital! That doctor would tell them just to show up whenever it was time…at the very least it would've been nice to have their records. It would've been nice to know how far along they were and what their labs looked like. Labor and Delivery is similar to an ER in that you can't turn patients away. They have to be evaluated first, no matter what.

We were also down the street from a birthing center, so we received all the failed midwife deliveries. I'm not knocking midwives or birthing centers, but it was *interesting* to say the least. Thank goodness we were right down the street, or there would have been some bad outcomes for their babies! You see, after you work labor and delivery for a while, there is no way you can have your baby at home; you know how wrong things can go in a matter of seconds.

Eventually, our labor and delivery shut down due to lack of payment from all the ER drop-in patients, and I moved to a larger hospital down in the Medical Center. Women's Hospital is the *bee's knees* of places to have your baby. We had approximately 1000 deliveries a month, and we cared for a lot of high-risk patients. If anything was going to go wrong in your delivery, this is where you wanted to be. The cool thing about Women's is it does not have an ER; therefore, there weren't any ambulances or ER drop-ins unless they were smarter than most and were able to manage their way in. Most patients had insurance too. A common question I received from fathers was, "And who will take our bags to our rooms for us?" Well, that would be you, sir.

This is still a hospital, not a five-star hotel. That was my favorite job of all time. The people were great, so was the atmosphere, and patient care was at its finest. My co-workers were like family, and they would be the ones to help me through the years to come.

Shortly after moving to Houston, Kevin and I began to have problems. I wouldn't call them BIG problems, but we had definitely drifted apart. There had been a change in the dynamics of our relationship. We were both feeling the stress with work, school, and kids. We had no family, and no help, other than the lady at preschool. Obviously, she was doing enough. His sister did live in Houston, but she was busy with her own life. Before long, we had both become so wrapped up in what we had going on, there wasn't much communication taking place at all. If I'm being honest, this was just as much my fault as his. It's hard to work full time, take care of kids, the house, yourself, and still find time for your husband at the end of the day. I was TIRED!   I could come up with 5,000 excuses right now, but I'll save that for a second book.   Point being, we were busy and were drifting further and further apart.

My sister-in-law had come to visit and brought to my attention some interesting information about my *not-so-fabulous* husband.  I was always under the impression that we were each other's "first." Wait for it… I was wrong once again.  He had lied to me about his past sexual history, before and while we were dating.  Apparently he was NOT the "virgin" he had originally claimed to be, shocking I know.  I confronted him, and after a lot of back and forth, the truth was finally revealed.   As a matter of fact, he had been with not one, not two, not five women before me, but TEN DIFFERENT WOMEN before he and I were ever together!  I also found out he had a threesome with one of my best friends in high school.  Say what?  *Ewww*.  That was a total slap in the face.  I remember feeling everything up to that point had been a lie.  If he'd lied about that, what else had he lied about? How could I trust him? It may not seem like such a big deal, but when you've been with the same person since you were 16, you expect both of you know about each other's pasts. We dated for two years before getting married and had been married for four years by that point. That is supposed to be one of the few bonuses to getting married young, knowing all about the other person's baggage.

Things grew worse from there. Months went by, and we barely spoke to each other. I honestly wanted out at that point. I know it seems minor in comparison to the other things I had heard about him, but I no longer trusted him. If you don't have trust, what do you have? The realization that there would always be skeletons in his closet was all too real. I loved him, but I was *tired* of being lied to. How hard is it to be honest? The cheating in high school, the lying about his sexual history, my friends he had slept with, and rumors of him continuing to cheating; it was all too much.

I tried talking to my mom and older sister about it, but neither of them wanted to hear it. They said I needed to find a way to work it out or try marriage counseling. They didn't really get it, but by that point, we did have two kids. I owed it to my children to try and work it out. So, that's exactly what I did. Loving someone is a *choice*. Making your marriage work is a *choice*. We all have options; it's what we choose to do with them that makes all the difference, right? We started going to marriage counseling and began working through our problems. Our counselor was great, and we both really liked her. We talked about *everything*: trust issues, the little things that drove us crazy, the things we wanted to improve, etc. Marriage counseling was a great experience; it seemed as though we were really getting somewhere. Up until that point, I hadn't really considered what I wanted or needed to be happy, I was just going through the motions, surviving day to day. We had to work on us. We started making a point to go on dates and making time for our relationship. It felt like we were finally on our way to a healthy, mature relationship. She gave us an assignment every week to work on, and by the time we were finished, we were on our way to a *rock solid* marriage. We were going to make this work, for better or for worse, right?

Here is where things really started to get interesting. Both of our girls had the stomach virus one weekend. Our youngest daughter was about 9-months-old at the time, she had woken up during the night, and desperate for some sleep, I put her in bed with me. Imagine it, here we are, sleeping face to face, with her head propped up on my arm. I had finally dozed back off when I was awakened with vomit hitting me in the face. This is no joke; it even went IN MY MOUTH! Motherhood -- the most rewarding and disgusting job there is. I jumped out of bed and was screaming for a towel. By the time I got all cleaned up, the opportunity for sleep had come and gone. Both girls were sick off and on the next day, and I hadn't been able to have much of a break at all. I was exhausted, outright disgusted, and needed a break! The stench had literally singed the hairs in my nostrils by this point. I needed to soak in a tub filled with the aroma of lavender, Lysol, bleach, or really anything else. I would've settled for a shower, new clothes and a sponge bath, fresh air, or frankly just a spray down with a can of Febreze. Anything at that point would've been accepted.

Kevin hadn't been much help at all, which really wasn't much of a shock by that point. He had developed a bit of a drinking problem, and he began helping less and less. He was busy; after all, he was in medical school, so I often let it slide. Once he started medical school, he had become a fairly absent father and husband, although the marriage counseling had helped. Kevin seemed to be trying; however, he had a big exam he was preparing for during this time. I went to look for him about 6 pm and much to my dismay, I found him sitting at the computer *jacking off to porn*. Really, porn? Dinner time.

6 pm. That's bold. I'm cleaning up after kids all evening long, and he's getting his kicks off to some stupid hoes on pornography sites. I was *LIVID*, to say the least. What a crappy excuse for a husband, not to mention a father! I didn't know what to think. I mean it's weird, who even does that?

That was not the first incident; unfortunately, there had been other times, I had also caught him in college. At the time, I thought it was because he was young and immature. When he would visit the strip club with friends, I thought it was just something guys did. Harmless enough, right? Naïve, I know. There's nothing *normal* or harmless about it. Was it really that common? Did he have a problem? I really had no idea. Is it cheating or not? Is it okay to get off to pictures or videos of other women when your wife is sitting in the other room? Truth of the matter is; it's *shocking* just how common it is. Pornography has become such an acceptable practice in our society, and it can lead to devastating results.

That was the beginning of an entirely different world. After that episode, I couldn't avoid the fact there were problems. I couldn't blame it on being young, friends, stress, or whatever other excuses he came up with. I just had no clue how deep our problems ran or what to do about them. Believe me, at this point, I know what you're thinking. And believe me, as I write it all down here – I'm thinking the same as you… idiot.

## *MEDICAL SCHOOL HAD ITS FLAWS*

During the second year of medical school, you are asked to be a mentor for incoming students. Kevin volunteered, and we were paired up with Rick and Christie, another young couple with a small child. We instantly hit it off. They were our best friends, and almost immediately, they were just like family. We spent every weekend together, took vacations together, and were basically inseparable. It was so much fun, and so nice to *finally* have a friend my age! It had been hard moving to Houston, I didn't know any other young mothers, and I didn't really have much of a support system. I finally had a person, she was my person I could trust and count on for everything. We would have cookouts, sing karaoke (usually after a series of drinks throughout the evening), and occasionally have a night out without kids.

We even went skiing to Tahoe and Taos with Rick and Christie. Christie and I had a great system. We would go to the bar, have a drink, head up the mountain and then have another drink as soon as we got back down. It was a blast! One time, she even decided she was done skiing about half way down the mountain; so, she just laid down. She laid there until the ski patrol came and got her and bought her down the mountain. She was *hilarious*.

It was during Kevin's senior year of medical school when the drinking really seemed to take a nosedive. It soon turned into everyone hanging out till 3 am; Kevin and Rick just wouldn't ever stop. I could put my girls to bed, go to bed myself, and they still kept going, or at least Kevin did. They would take Xanax, Vicodin, anything really, along with their beer or whatever else they were drinking. Kevin got to where he couldn't quit. Every weekend was the same thing: drinking, taking pills, up all night, etc. Things were spiraling out of control! It wasn't fun anymore. In fact, it began to feel out right childish. We were grown adult, with children. Things had to change. I loved this other couple, but it was beginning to be a *problem*; especially, when I became pregnant with our 3rd child. It isn't fun to be the only sober one in the room, especially when you're pregnant, tired, and taking care of a 3 and 6-year-old.

It was the February of Kevin's last semester in medical school (remember, I'm pregnant and taking care of two other kids) and the weekend of my oldest daughter's birthday party. Kevin had gone over to our friends' house with Rick and

Christie, after the party, along with another couple. My family was in town, and I wasn't feeling too well (gotta love that 1st trimester nausea), so I stayed home with my other two children. They had all spent the evening playing poker and drinking. Kevin ended up getting in fairly late; the next day I called Christie, and was surprised with the information she shared with me. I was absolutely heartbroken. Apparently, Kevin had started calling her the week before, when I was out of town. He wanted them to get together and "hang out." She didn't really think much of it because we were all such close friends; however, the night before he apparently attempted to *kiss* her in HER driveway. It was insane, and frankly, the *last* thing I had expected to hear. Seriously, she was one of my BEST friends! She was my person. I was so angry, and hurt.

When I questioned Kevin, he, of course, denied it. He acted like she was *crazy* and had no idea why she would say such a thing. He even went so far as to get on the phone with her and tell her he found her disgusting and she was one of the last people he would try and get with. He said she was jealous of us, of what we had. I didn't know who to believe, my best friend or my husband? I mean, I knew whom to believe. Talk about being stuck between a rock and a hard place. I wouldn't say I thought she was lying, but I chose to end the friendship and stand by my husband. Again, I know, you're probably *cussing* me by this point. If I had chosen her, where would we go from there? How do you remain friends and move forward as couples? I couldn't fathom the thought of him trying to make a move on one of my best friends, especially with her husband right around the corner. I chalked it up to her being dramatic, and frankly, I was sick of all the late nights. Christie wasn't able to let it go as easily. She didn't understand why we couldn't all work through it, she hadn't done anything wrong, she was honest with me, and loved me like a sister. After several weeks of going back and forth with Rick and Christie, our friendship was severed. I was really sad, and I *hated* losing a friend. She was basically like family; I was even her labor nurse with her 2nd child. We did everything together, and a part of me will always miss her. I just didn't see how we could continue our friendship at this point; I mean how do you move forward? Here I was, pregnant with our 3rd child, I guess it was just easier to believe him. I think this is why so many people stay with their cheating husbands. It wasn't enough to end our marriage, and frankly, I was tired. Who am I kidding, it was more than enough to end our marriage, but I didn't. I was working full time and taking care of 2 other children, and I just didn't have the energy to deal with it. I didn't know if I could afford it, and I didn't want to share my babies. It was honestly going to take something much bigger than that for me to end my marriage.

One night, a friend of mine was staying the night, and Kevin began ringing the doorbell repeatedly. He had been outside watering the lawn and had apparently taken Xanax while drinking beer all evening. He was in a panic and thought the grass was talking to him. No, I am not exaggerating, like I said, I really can't make this stuff up. My girlfriend about fell on the ground laughing. After all, here he was, a doctor, thinking the grass was taking to him! We were hysterical. Honestly, neither one of us thought much of it at the time. Having grown up fairly sheltered, I had no clue what a problem he had. I had never even known anyone with a drug or drinking problem. Unfortunately, this wasn't the only incident, there were way too many to account for.

Another stand out moment was when my mom was in town. Kevin had been outside all day working on something, I can't recall exactly what, but I do remember it was in the middle of the day. As my mother and I were leaving with the girls, we looked over while he was attempting to put his shoe on. Right at that moment, he FACE PLANTED into the corner of the brick lining the flowerbed and knocked himself out.

He was *completely* trashed. After that, my mom attempted to bring up his drinking. She was concerned; I on the other hand, didn't see it, or didn't want to. What was I going to do about it? Looking back, I see this was a repetitive theme for me.

The drinking continued throughout medical school and into residency. I knew he was drinking *a lot*, and I knew it was a problem, I just didn't know what to do about it. Every time I said something he would tell me how he was finally in his last year of medical school and was just trying to relax and have a good time. Makes sense enough right? Sure, whatever. I'm freaking tired, I've obviously let everything else go up to this point, why stop now?

Kevin had begun applying for residencies that December. He had gone to New York and some neighboring states for several interviews. He would usually visit his brother and his family when he went. One weekend, I flew to New York and met him after one of his interviews.

We stayed with his brother and sister-in-law and their two kids. I love both of them. All in all, it was a good visit, if you don't count the fact that the entire time I felt like he and his sister-in-law were together and I was the 3rd wheel. Sounds strange, I know; try being there. Something was off, I'm not a jealous person either, it was just that *obvious,* and that weird. They were constantly touching and laughing with each other, almost like they had their own inside jokes. We even went shopping one day while his brother was at work, and he stayed with her the entire time while I shopped by myself. I kept trying to convince myself I was being paranoid or ridiculous or something. Unsure if I was losing my mind, I finally confronted him about the possibility of something going on between them. Deny! Deny! Deny! Looking back, I realize you should always go with your gut instinct! If it looks like a duck, swims like a duck, and quacks like a duck, then it probably is a duck. My sister-in-law did tell me later that they were in fact having an affair. So, I'm not entirely crazy.

What's crazy is the fact I was still with him, blinders on and all.

My family takes a vacation together every summer; from the time I was a small child up through adulthood. As adults, there had been years my sisters or I had to miss for various reasons, but for the most part, we all tried to make it as it gave us a great chance to catch up. I'm lucky that I have a very close family and we actually enjoy being around each other. Some of my best childhood memories involve a pop up trailer, a KOA campground, and entirely too many hours jammed in the back of an Astro Minivan. We drove all over the U.S. in the summer to go on vacation. To save money, my parents always packed an ice chest, and we always camped. My sweet mom would actually cook hot dogs by placing them on the windshield wrapped in a piece of foil. We make fun of her now, but it actually worked pretty well.

The summer after Kevin graduated from medical school, before starting residency, we went on vacation with my entire family.  I was pregnant with our 3rd child, due at the end of August, so we weren't able to travel too far.  We stayed at a resort on a lake in Texas.  As usual, Kevin had *too much* to drink.  It was embarrassing, here we are, having our 3rd child, he's a physician, I'm a nurse, and he can't even have one evening of responsible drinking.  My family questioned me about whether or not he had a problem.  This wasn't the first time they'd brought it up either (my family is not one to get in the middle of each other's problems either.  Bringing it up was uncomfortable for them, to say the least).  He told me he had been stressed out and was just trying to relax and everything was fine.  He told me not to worry; we were good, and he didn't have a problem.  I knew there was more to it, but I just didn't know how to handle it.  Other than him drinking a little too much, I thought everything was fine.  I am the queen of keeping my nose to the grind.  I'm a worker; I am not one of those girls who sit around and think about all the attention I'm not getting.  In my mind, we were both busy, he with school and me with work and the kids. We were about to have our 3rd child, a boy, we had just bought a new house in the 'burbs, he had finished medical school, and he was about to start his residency. Overall, I thought things were going pretty well and keeping in theme, I chose to ignore the "*binge*" drinking! Yes, yes. I realize it's not binge if it's 24/7. As if that wasn't the most embarrassing part, I later found out he had stolen my mom's pain pills she was taking for her recent knee surgery. My parents found them hidden in a towel in the bathroom we were using. I guess it's hard to be a responsible drinker when you're doped up. Pills + Alcohol = reckless. Not that it really should have been a surprise to me by that point.

The day had finally arrived for our son to be born. Kevin had been on call the night before, so he met me at the hospital. Everything went great, it was my third cesarean section, so we were pretty much pros by that point. The delivery was full of all my friends and favorite docs and co-workers. My son was born on my favorite scrub tech's birthday, intentionally as planned by my OB and the scrub tech. Everything went great; Kevin stayed with me while I was in the hospital, and my mom stayed with the kids. My mom had to leave the day I was discharged from the hospital to go back to work. We moved the week before I delivered into our new house, so she had already been off a week to come help me. So here I was; me and three kids, with no help. Kevin had just started residency and was gone *ALL* the time. If he wasn't working, he was moon lighting (which is a way for residents to make extra money when hospitals are short-handed). Luckily, I felt pretty good; honestly I surprised myself at how well I was able to manage it all.

I was about 5 days post-delivery, when we decided to get out of the house. I had been cooped up with 3 kids, and we weren't going to survive each other the next week if we didn't get out for a little fun. We went for Mexican food and played putt-putt. I thought it would be good to take the girls out to do something fun with all the new changes; after all they were 4 and 7 by this point. The only problem was Kevin drank so much at dinner; I had to drive home, put him to bed, and take the kids by myself. Awesome, five days post cesarean: driving, and putt-putt alone with a newborn, 4, and 7-year-old. I guess I could've just stayed home, but I wasn't about to disappoint my children. Someone has to be the parent, and as usual, that would be me. This was becoming an all too frequent event, and I had no clue how to handle it! What happened to the loving husband and father that had been my partner back in Lubbock? Over the last 4 years he had disappeared. There was no explanation, and I was living in my own personal hell.

## RED FLAGS:

1. Look at their family; odds are most people are going to turn out exactly like their parents. The expression *"the apple doesn't fall far from the*

*tree*" definitely has some truth to it! Pay attention ladies, you will not change them!

2. If your family doesn't like them, it should tell you something. Your family has your best interest at heart. If he were such a great guy, why wouldn't they want you to be with them? Listen to their points at the very least!

3. Once a cheater always a cheater! People don't change and you aren't going to change them. The problem is if you put up with it, they think you always will and will continue to do it. Also, if he cheated on a past girlfriend with you, why wouldn't he do the same thing to you? Any relationship that begins with cheating is more than likely going to end the same way.

4. If something seems too good to be true, it probably is. We are all human, and Lord knows we all have our flaws, figure out what theirs are and if they're something you can tolerate. If you don't see any, there's a problem.

5. Pornography is not normal. While it may be acceptable, think about all that it can lead to. What's next: swinging, threesomes, prostitution, escort services? Things that may not seem like a problem while you're dating can be a huge problem later.

6. Binge drinking actually isn't normal. All teenagers don't do it, all college kids don't do it, and it can actually be a sign of a drinking problem or addiction, especially if there is a family history.

7. Rumors don't get started completely out of the blue. Maybe they could be an exaggerated version of the truth, but they came from something. Don't be so quick to dismiss it, investigate it. If it walks like a duck, swims like a duck, and quacks like a duck, then it's probably a duck.

8. If they say they are always working, make sure there's a paycheck to match the hours. Pay attention to the world around you. Life is not

just about working and moving forward from one task to another, running from one event or game to the next. Don't forget to enjoy it. Don't forget to pay attention. Stop turning a blind eye.

# WHEN THINGS WENT SOUTH

*MY EYES WERE FINALLY OPENED.....TO A HOOKER*

It was 5 am when I woke up to the cries of my youngest child. Kevin had been on call the night before and slept all day (he had just started his first month of residency). I realized he had never come to bed that night. I placed my 3 month old in his swing and turned on the ceiling fan, as I did every morning. He could watch the ceiling fan for hours. As I walked towards the back door, I noticed it was cracked and I *heard* a woman's voice. I poked my head outside, and there was my husband…with another woman… in the act.

I quickly shut the door, trying to process what I had just witnessed and how I was going to deal with it. I was paralyzed, numb of emotion, and it took everything I had to even move. I even went so far as to go to my bedroom and put on a pair of pants. All I could think was how I wished I had stayed asleep and never seen that. I didn't want to deal; I mean I was still on maternity leave! I was supposed to be focusing on adjusting to a new baby, not a cheating husband!

As I sat there, replaying what I had just witnessed, I gathered up the strength to confront him. I'm sure you are sitting there thinking about how you would kill him, attack him with your bare hands, cut his dick off—that's what I always thought as well. As I was standing there, completely blindsided, it took all I had to put one foot in front of the other and confront him. My world, as I knew it, had just blown up right in my face. I flipped on the light, walked outside, and screamed... *"What the fuck is going on out here?"* To which she quickly threw her hands up, collected her $500, and left. As my husband sat there, pants around his ankles, used condom still on, I realized that my *entire* marriage had been a lie. I didn't even know him; I had been married to a complete stranger-- and that's when my eyes were finally open wide.

Kevin just sat there, dumfounded, asking me what I was talking about. I mean I may have been blind up to this point, but really? I quickly ripped the condom off and shoved it in his mouth, used and all. That's what I'm talking about, asshole! I stormed off in disbelief. My entire world as I knew it was over, crumbling around me, and nothing would ever be the same. He followed me into the house, muttering something about how I didn't touch him enough, he needed attention (apparently), and then quickly passed out on the couch. All I knew at that point was I had to get out of there, so I packed up my three kids and headed to my sister's in Dallas. Kevin's problems were obviously *much* deeper than I had ever realized.

I definitely don't believe God has anything to do with situations like that occurring, but I do believe he prepares you, and here's how. I had packed my car up the night before, knowing it would be difficult to pack everyone up and get to my sister's at a decent time with a newborn.

Thank God I had too! I had already planned on going to Dallas the following day for my nephew's birthday. After catching Kevin, I was distraught. It would have been nearly impossible for me to arrive with half of what we needed at that point. Before I loaded the kids in the car, I called my sister and best friend— I had to tell someone what had happened.

My sister and my best friend were shocked to hear I had caught Kevin with a hooker on the back porch. Needless to say, I was beside myself and they were speechless. It's one of those life shattering moments none of us will ever forget. You know what I'm talking about, when a tragedy occurs, and you will always clearly remember where you were and what you were doing in that exact moment of time—like when 911 occurred, or President Kennedy was shot, something Earth shattering! Clearly *"I just caught Kevin on the back porch with a hooker,"* was a sentence I *never* anticipated saying in my life. They both asked, "What!?" multiple times, partially because I was sobbing and couldn't quite speak clearly, and partly because they were in disbelief.

By the time I reached Dallas, my sister had called my *entire* family and a couple of my close friends, including my grandmothers, and filled them in on all the details. Thank you big sister! As if the situation wasn't humiliating enough, let's fill in the 86-year-old grandmothers. Awesome!

By the time I arrived, they were all either there or on their way. We all talked and cried for a long time while the kids played outside; amazingly, I was able to keep it together in front of my children and they didn't have the slightest clue there was a problem. Luckily for me, I have an amazing support system, people willing to stand behind whatever decision I make. I can remember my father saying, *"We will support whatever decision you make, but I'm telling you right now, people like that don't change."*

At that point, I had no clue what I wanted or what I was going to do. All I could think was how unfair it was. I was going to have to give up holidays, summers, and birthdays just because he was a dumbass that couldn't keep it in his pants. Really? It wasn't fair! I didn't want to share my kids! This wasn't my plan, and all around, it was a bunch of crap.

## *ALCOHOLICS: TO BINGE OR NOT TO BINGE*

After not speaking for several weeks, I was finally willing to meet with Kevin. He told me he thought he was an alcoholic and he had been abusing prescription medications. He would down a 12 pack of beer on his way home from work, chase it with Xanax, drink some more, and then go to bed. When he drank crown and coke, he would drink an *entire* bottle! Drugs of choice: Xanax, Ambien, hydrocodone, and those were just the ones I knew about.

Whenever Kevin wasn't going to be working the following day, he would sit up the entire night drinking. He told me about how pornography on the computer had eventually turned into ordering an adult escort to our house. For the past several years, Kevin had been leaving our home in the middle of the night to drive to massage parlors, in order to pay for sexual favors, mainly blowjobs! How could I have missed all of this? It was like I wasn't even in the same marriage. I knew he was drinking a lot, but I had no idea how deep his issues ran.

Kevin told me his friends did the same thing, and that's how he learned about the massage parlors. I felt like I was in a bad episode of Law and Order: SVU, and I was cracking the case. I'm a total Law and Order: SVU addict. I think in a different life, that's totally what I would be; only I'd be a detective, NOT the *dumbass* wife of the alleged perp.

We went to church every Sunday, we had three beautiful children and he was now a physician FOR CRYING OUT LOUD!! I was dumbfounded, to say the least. This WAS NOT the way it was supposed to be. This wasn't my plan. How do you get through something of this magnitude? What is the other side?

We continued talking, and after several months, Kevin moved back in. Most addicts are great manipulators; although, I don't know that I needed much manipulating. After all, we had three kids together, the youngest being a couple months old. Kevin was sick, he needed help; obviously, because who in their right mind would do the things he had done? I know it sounds crazy, but I felt like it was my job to help him.

Nurses are the absolute worst about wanting to fix people. We think we can change them; we can make the difference. *"The martyr sacrifices themselves entirely in vain or rather not in vain; for they make the selfish more selfish, the lazy more lazy, the narrow narrower"* – Florence Nightingale.

Kevin had begun attending some Alcoholics Anonymous meetings, however, the drinking continued.  He also said he was going to counseling.  Every 2-3 weeks I would get home from work and he would be stumbling, falling down drunk.  Home alone with the kids, insisting he hadn't had a drop to drink.  He would even come home drunk from his AA meeting, and tell me I was crazy for thinking he was drinking.

I would search the house inside and out.  Finally, when I would find evidence of his drinking, only then would he finally own up to it.  It was insane.  Then it was my fault because I wasn't attending meetings with him.  I wasn't supportive enough.  *Never* his fault, always mine.   Well you big idiot, who has your kids while you're at these "alleged meetings?'  ME, that's who.

Every time I came home, I had a terrible, sick feeling in my gut, wondering what I would be coming home to.  Would my kids be ok?  Had he already sent the sitter home?  Was he too messed up to care for the baby?  This continued on and on, and of course, I let it.   Kevin would only admit to any drinking or prescription drug abuse when he was caught red handed.   I was beginning to be unable to tell the difference between the smell of alcohol and the smell of mouthwash!  I bet he drank a bottle of mouthwash a day, at least!  I knew this wasn't going to be easy, I knew he needed help.  I mean, at least he was trying right?  Two steps forward, three steps back.

## *CHRISTMAS AT BERNIES*

I will NEVER forget my first Christmas with Kevin once we got back together. It was memorable, to say the least.  It was Christmas Eve, and Kevin, the kids, my little sister, and I were meeting his family at the Toyota Center for a Christmas Eve service.  I believe it was for the Second Baptist Church, where his sister was a member.  Clint Black was singing, and there was a turnout in the hundreds of thousands.

Kevin *insisted* on dropping off me, my sister, and the kids at the door so he could find a parking space.  It gave me an odd feeling, but I went along with it. We got inside, met his family, and all found our seats up in the nosebleed section.

An hour later, Kevin still hadn't shown up. I was beginning to get nervous. Finally, he called, and my sister went out to meet him in the lobby, where he began staggering towards her. Somehow she got Kevin up the escalator, and brought him to our seats by holding his limp body to her chest and dragging him down the aisle. I was *humiliated*!

Kevin reeked of alcohol; apparently he drank an entire bottle of Crown Royal in the parking lot before coming in! I stared at him, disgusted, and wondered what the hell was wrong with him. It was Christmas for Pete's sake, and we were at church!

The offering plates began traveling up and down the aisles, and before I knew it, Kevin had grabbed one and made it his own personal vomit bowl. That's right. He began puking in front of EVERYONE at the service. Kevin then passed out on my sister's shoulder (to which I thought…Thank God people think he's with her) and then he began throwing up on her too! We couldn't get him to wake up after the service. It was like the movie Weekend at Bernie's, only, unfortunately, he wasn't dead!

The only information we could get out of him was he had no idea where he had parked my car in downtown Houston. It was *humiliating*! People were staring, my kids were pointing and laughing at him! My sister and brother-in-law managed to carry Kevin out of the Toyota Center and into the parking garage, *yelling* at preachers and police officers on the way to please not help them, he was just ill.

When they finally made it to his sister's car, Kevin DROPPED HIS PANTS and PEED in front of every minivan passing by. Wow, what a winner and *great example* for my children. My sister and brother-in-law then threw him in the trunk, pants around his ankles, and drove him to his sister's house. After walking around downtown Houston for what felt like hours, Kevin's sister and I finally found the car. We loaded everyone up, and headed home. Merry freaking Christmas to me!

## *THE DRINK GOES ON...AND ON...AND ON*

The drinking continued off and on for another 6 months. Kevin had a friend from high school come in town on business, and he needed a place to stay. Kevin and his friend went to the store, and when they returned, I learned they had loaded up on beer…. pissed off does not even begin to describe my reaction!!! Kevin was *supposed* to have quit drinking, still claiming to be a *"recovering alcoholic."*

I finally went to bed, trying not to make a scene in front of our friend; but how dare he! What a slap in the face, after all I had forgiven him for; hadn't Kevin put me through enough? As the night continued on, Kevin became out of control as usual. He even tried calling the escort service, again. Lucky for him, his friend stopped him, but he did call me the next day. He didn't realize how out of control and what a problem Kevin had, and he thought Kevin needed rehab. Me and you both buddy, good luck with that!!

After finding out about the attempt to get another hooker, I was done. I told Kevin I wanted out. I couldn't do it any longer. I was just *tired*. It would've been hard enough to move forward without the drinking.

He begged and pleaded for me to stay. Kevin promised me the next time he drank, he would move out willingly and be agreeable to whatever I decided. Kevin told me he loved me more than I would ever know; I was the only person that had ever loved him unconditionally. I had always been there, always the rock. He needed me. So I thought…why not? I'll catch him again in two weeks, tops! If he hadn't changed by that point, I knew NOTHING would change him.

It had been almost a year, and there were *no signs* of Kevin drinking. Our relationship wasn't great, but we were chugging along. I had a hard time wanting to spend time with him, much less be intimate with him. I tried to put the hooker incident and all the pain that came along with it behind me. Although I didn't bring it up, it was always in the back of my mind. I don't know how you can cheat and ever earn that trust back, especially after hurting someone that deeply. Maybe if you saw a change in their actions, but there was no foreseeable change.

Kevin was more selfish than ever. He was always at the gym, working, at a meeting, or out with his "AA buddies." He rarely spent time with me, or the kids. Kevin said he needed it for his mental wellbeing. He was trying to stay clean, and I wanted to make it as easy as possible for him. I wanted him to be well and to be the leader of our household that God intended.

Meanwhile, I was working full-time and taking care of the house, yard, and kids all by myself. Half the time, I wasn't sure why I was still there and I prayed about it all the time. I prayed that if he was never going to really change, God would give me a sign. I prayed that I could truly forgive him and move forward, and I prayed we would be a family like we used to be. I prayed that none of this had ever happened but since it had, God, please make it better. Help me to be happy, whatever His will may be.

It wasn't like I didn't have enough reasons to leave. I felt it was right to leave the last time I caught him drinking, but I needed more. We were growing further and further apart. I knew things weren't right. I wasn't happy, he wasn't happy, we weren't close, and the friendship we'd once shared had dissipated.

Our nanny, who had been a Godsend at the time, moved. We had found a replacement, although things weren't really working out. She was *awful,* and the kids couldn't stand her. She was mean, and half the time, wouldn't even buckle them in a seat belt. The last straw was when my daughter told me she vomited in her oatmeal and the sitter made her eat it anyway. That was it!

I needed to find someone new, and I knew the perfect person, my little sister. She moved in with us that May. She wanted to go back to school and kept the kids for me on the days I worked. It was a PERFECT solution for both of us. Who better to keep your kids than your sister? It's funny how things work out, I *never* would have made it through what was to come without her! God will always prepare us for what is to come; He will never give us more than we can handle.

I was at my sisters in Dallas, and Kevin had stayed back in Houston (he had to work, and frankly, things were uncomfortable when he was around my family). He had gone to an Astros game with some friends. He called me at midnight, after the game, saying he couldn't find where he parked his car. It was in a parking garage in downtown Houston somewhere. Very helpful, I know. I told him I didn't know how to help; after all, I was in Dallas.

I asked Kevin if he'd been drinking, because he sounded like it, and of course he denied it. His mother was in Houston at the time visiting his sister, so he called her. She and his brother-in-law came, found him, and drove him around to find his truck. The only bad thing, he later told me, was that while he was waiting for them, he *literally* crapped his pants, and it stunk to high heaven!!

I know what you're thinking, who craps their pants? Truth be told, Kevin had crapped his pants our first day at Tech and had done it twice a year for the past 10 years, that I knew about. The past couple of years, it became more frequent, probably twice a month he would literally crapped in his pants. Causes? Drugs, alcohol, prescription medications, anal sex? Who the hell knows what Kevin was in to? All I know is that he crapped his pants. *A LOT.* What to do? Wear Depends? He would've never gone for that!

We went to Disney World that summer and met my other sister and her family out there. The trip was beyond miserable. Kevin and I had gotten into a fight before we left, and he wouldn't speak to me the entire trip. Seriously, we drove from Texas to Florida and never spoke. Not a single word, unless there was no other option, as in, "*I need a potty break.*"

We spent a week in Florida and only discussed the kids. We drove home, and never spoke once! He was constantly on his phone texting. While we were in Florida, I told my sister I suspected he was having an affair; not drinking like the time before, just cheating. You know that sinking feeling in the pit of your stomach that I'm talking about. You know something is off, but you can't quite put your finger on it. You can't catch him; you can't prove it.

I think when someone is cheating; the signs are all there. You know what I'm referring to, ladies. He hides his text messages, spends more time on the phone, puts passwords on the computer, and spends more time on it; he's more distant, and best of all, he has to work more.

I confronted Kevin when we got back, but of course, he denied it. I just didn't have the energy to dig further. I have always believed if someone is cheating on you, you will eventually catch him. It may take 10 years, but it will *eventually* happen. After all, I'd caught him before, hadn't I? Truly, I sound pathetic. How little you must care for someone to not put forth enough effort to figure out if they are cheating. I think the past 10 years had been such a beat down, that at that point, I really just didn't care. I was working 60 hours a week and taking care of 3 kids, there was nothing left to give a rat's ass.

## THE STRAW THAT FINALLY BROKE THE CAMEL

It was August, the weekend before school started back. I came home from work that afternoon and was looking through the yard at the sprinkler system. It had a leak, and a friend of mine had suggested some ways to find it. Kevin sure as hell wasn't ever going to get around to doing anything about it.

My little sister had come outside to help me. Just as I rounded the bushes in the front, I saw an empty 12 pack of beer. She could read the look all over my face. THAT WAS IT! I was done! I knew in my heart at that very moment the right thing to do was leave.

Here I was, working overtime that day, while Kevin sat at home, hiding and drinking. What a stand-up guy. I didn't have a doubt in my mind THEN and never have since. I guess it was almost a relief, really. I had known things were off; now I knew I had been right. I had my sister take the kids to get ice cream while I confronted Kevin. He denied drinking, of course, but I laid out all the empty bottles on the counter, and he was forced to admit it.

I told him that I wanted a divorce. As I was leaving, he began chasing me across the front yard. Luckily, I made it to the car and was able to lock the door. I backed out of my driveway with him beating on the windows *screaming* at me. Very classy, I know, no doubt the neighbors got a good show! The kids and I stayed at a friend's house that night, where we received multiple drunken, threatening phone calls. The calls, of course, didn't start until he got home from a party one of his friends was having. Kevin left me voicemails saying he was going to call and report us for kidnapping if we didn't bring the kids back immediately. A million texts and calls later, he must've finally passed out.

It was finally over, I felt like a weight had been lifted off my shoulders. Years of not knowing what I was going to come home to, worrying about what shape he was in while caring for our children, trying to get over all the hurt and pain, but knowing deep inside nothing was really different, I didn't have to do it anymore. No more fake it till you make it. Hasta La Vista Baby!

We went home the next day. I called Kevin that morning and told him he had two options; he could leave on his own, or we would go to Dallas. He agreed to leave if we would at least stay in Houston. When we arrived, Kevin told the kids he was moving out, packed up his stuff, and left. High drama. He was crying, they were crying. Frankly, I was just *annoyed*. You brought this on yourself, no one feels sorry for you, and your drama-filled performance is just upsetting the kids. Seriously, leave. We told them it was because he had a drinking problem, that's what we told them after the hooker incident, too. We had tried to work it out but were unable to. Of course they were upset at first, but I think they had somewhat expected it after everything they'd witnessed the previous two years. Kids are observant, they see and understand a lot more than we give them credit for.

It's odd, but since the day Kevin moved out, the kids never asked if we could get back together, not even once. They've never begged to see him, for us to be a family, nothing. That speaks volumes!

## PREPARING TO LEAVE YOUR OWN PERSONAL HELL

The best advice I could ever give someone is to wait until you're ready. It's like when you go into labor; you will know when it's time. You won't have to second-guess yourself; it will slap you in the face like a brick wall. Don't leave before you're ready either, unless of course you're in a violent or dangerous situation. That wasn't the case for me; I'd stayed for over a year after the "hooker" incident. I prayed about it all the time. Looking back, I don't know if it was God telling me not to give up on my marriage yet, if I just wasn't ready to, or if I was just scared. Regardless, I needed to stay and try to work it out. I had to know I had tried *everything* before I could give up. I never wanted to look back with any regret, and I never have. When I left my husband, I knew without a doubt in my mind I had tried everything possible. I knew Kevin would never change, at least not while he was with me. I truly felt at peace with my decision and like God was telling me it was okay. I had tried and done what I could, and it was time. I do not take divorce lightly. I was raised to believe, and still do, that a commitment of marriage is forever. Unfortunately, we are sometimes in relationships that are unhealthy and we aren't left with much of an option. It makes me sick to think about what all my children and I would've been exposed to if we had stayed.

Things I wish I would've done before the separation:

1.     Set some money aside. It doesn't have to be a large amount, just enough to get you through a hard spot because, believe me, it is coming. Don't put it in a bank account that can be associated with your name whatsoever or be traced back to you. Pull it out in cash, like when you're at the grocery store, and keep it hidden somewhere or have a family member or friend open an account in their name.

2.    Gather any evidence you can.  Get photos if they're cheating, screen shot their Facebook page, etc.  Look for any bank account information you have.  Know what you have financially and what you don't.  Keep a journal of anything suspicious.  Divorce can get nasty really quickly.  Maybe you won't have to resort to using any of this information, but if you do, then at least you will have it to use to your advantage.

3.    If there has been any abuse, get photos and go to the ER.  Documented medical records can be used in court for restraining orders, and most importantly, should there be a custody battle.

4.  Don't cover for them, don't be scared for them to get caught.  Letting him get arrested at the church service could have been a game changer.  It could've forced him into rehab.  It would've given me leverage in my divorce.  Who knows what other situations I am unaware of that it could've altered.

5. Have a plan. Know who you can count on, who will be your support system. If not your family, maybe a close friend? Luckily for me, I had my sister. It truly takes a village; don't be too proud to ask. My plan was to remain in Houston; however, the divorce became so volatile, my plans had to change. Having the support of my family made that possible.

# THE BIG D

I wasn't sure I had the energy to go through with a divorce, but I knew I couldn't stay. Dealing with Kevin had become unbearable. He had become increasingly _psychotic_ as time went on. I probably received at least 40 text messages a day telling me what a sinner I was for divorcing him, quoting bible verses, and calling me all kinds of everything under the sun. Seriously? Stop. You're going to quote scripture to me? You're a hooker fu*%#r!! Let's get real here and call a spade a spade. It was mentally _exhausting_.

Kevin began showing up, unannounced, demanding to take the kids whenever he pleased. It didn't matter what we were doing or what we had planned. It didn't matter how my babies felt. They would be crying, screaming they didn't want to go, and he didn't care. He didn't care about anyone but himself. It was all about what he wanted, what he needed, and what was convenient for him; just like the last half of our marriage. He would physically drag them out of the house and then let them repeatedly call me, crying that they wanted to come home. Pure torture.

He would hack my emails, voicemails, and anything he could get his hands on. Kevin had become obsessive. This was during the time MySpace was big. Whatever my profile song was, he would play it repeatedly while he had the kids. They weren't allowed to listen to anything else. Whenever they would get home and that song came on, they would yell, *"Change it, we can't listen to that anymore, dad made us listen to it over and over!"* So, I would change it, and the next weekend he had them the same thing would happen.

Not only did most of his texts include scripture, they also included entertaining criticism such as my absolute favorite, *"I made a reservation for you and your sister at the fat farm, don't keep them waiting."* He was completely out of control.

It was everyday ALL. Day. Long. It was so exhausting, and truly a mental beating! We were all constantly walking on eggshells, waiting for the next shoe to drop, waiting for his next attack, and trying to be prepared as much as possible. Like that was possible.

Kevin had stopped all checks coming into our account immediately. He had just taken out one last student loan to pay off the credit card bills he had racked up from the previous time we split up. Instead of paying any of that off, he took the money and pocketed it, leaving me to deal with the debt on top of everything else.

He didn't help with any bills or any other expenses for that matter either. Nada, zilch, didn't give a penny towards one bill, food for his kids, nothing. I was struggling financially and had nothing left in the account. Kevin even took my first paycheck after he left to put down as a deposit on his new apartment. Yes, I got my own account that very day, but that did not help buy food or anything else, and it would be another two weeks before we would get another check. I eventually got that money back after my mother gave his mother an earful…and that was the end of their friendship.

It was sad because our mothers had been best friends since we were children. My mother just couldn't handle the way he was treating the kids and I, or his mother's justifications for it. I was working overtime but still couldn't manage to pay all the bills. Between babysitting, utilities, house payment, etc., there wasn't enough money to go around. Nurses make good money, but considering it took both our incomes to pay everything prior to the split, one income wasn't going to cut it. My parents came in town and bought groceries when they could, but it was still a *struggle*. I had to do something, so my dad and I went and saw an attorney.

We met with an attorney a friend had recommended. She seemed very knowledgeable and told me what we needed to do to proceed with the divorce. She told me everything we were going to get and take him for, and really reassured me about the entire process. First, a non-refundable $3800 retainer fee was required and then we would file. We paid the money and left feeling confident we were on the right track.

One month later, the attorney STILL hadn't filed any papers with the court system. I couldn't get her or anyone in her office to return any of my phone calls, not to mention no one was ever at the office! Mistake #1: Don't hire the 1st attorney you meet with and make sure you do your research on her. I was so frustrated! Kevin was continuing harassing me, all the while not forking over a penny to help with any bills or costs of the children. There were no set temporary orders, child support, visitation, nothing. He could do whatever he wanted, take whatever he wanted, not help pay a *damn* thing, and there was nothing I could do about it. I was forced to eat the retainer fee and hire another attorney. What else could I do? We had to do something, temporary orders, set visitation, something.

The papers were finally filed, and Kevin and his attorney counter filed for full custody, though he claimed to have no idea why his attorney did that. Yeah right!!! Attorneys don't do anything without your knowledge and consent. I was livid. How *dare* he go for full custody after everything he had put me and the kids through? The fight was on. I was ready to call in any witness necessary to testify to his character, including family. I would stop at nothing to make sure I had my kids and that he would have as little exposure to them as possible.

I called his sister, and that didn't go over well AT ALL. She was *so mad* at me. After everything he had put the kids and I through, I couldn't imagine anyone being supportive of his behavior. I was floored to be honest. I know blood is thicker than water, but come on! It really hadn't occurred to me up to this point that his family would side with him. We had been married 10 years, and I had known them since childhood. Nope, they didn't care what he had put me through! They did not care one bit he was an alcoholic and a prescription drug addict. Worse than that, they obviously didn't care what he might expose my children to or if he would be incapacitated when he had them. As long as he got what he wanted, that's all that ever mattered. Always remember, no matter what they put you through or do to you, their family will always choose their side regardless. I was willing to do whatever it would take to keep my babies with me. I didn't know what he was up to, and frankly, I was scared. At this point I felt he was capable of anything and would have no qualms about crossing any moral boundaries. I don't think he even had moral boundaries. He actually meets 19 of the 20 indicators of a sociopath. Needless to say, I was *terrified*. He was a monster and I was in for the fight of my life.

Things continued on as before. I was still getting nasty texts on a regular basis throughout the day.

Kevin was still not giving any money to the kids or me. My sister was still living with me, and had taken a part time job to try and help out with the bills. We weren't making it though, and eventually had to quit making the house payments. Up to that point, I'd always had good credit, but when it comes to choosing between utilities and groceries versus a house payment, was there really an option? My parents were already helping with attorney fees and I couldn't ask them for any more money. I was biding my time, hoping to get a court date soon and move back to the small town where I grew up. My original plan was to stay in Houston, but after all that had happened, I realized there was no way I could make it. There was no way I would ever be able to count on him, I would always struggle, and the harassment would continue as long as I was there. My sister agreed to stay with me until I could move, but she couldn't handle any more either. Kevin may have been even more hateful to my little sister than he was to me. He was a complete psycho. Words cannot describe the hell he put us through. We were scared of him, and my kids were scared of him. We were running out of options, and moving back closer to my parents seemed like the only one we had.

As the harassment continued, Kevin and my sister even got in screaming arguments. He was constantly threatening to file charges against her so she couldn't babysit anymore. He would refuse to give the kids back and would tell me if I wanted them back I could come and get them. I would have to go to his apartment and wait for the gate to open because he wouldn't give me the code, nor would he come open it. When I got there, all I would hear was how fat and disgusting I was, how nobody would ever want me with 3 kids, and how I needed to get to the gym. It was *miserable*; he was an ass. I wanted my kids with me as much as possible, I thought the less time they were with him, the better, so we would endure the abuse. We would sit outside his gate sometimes 30 minutes or more; whatever it took to get my babies back.

Kevin would take the kids camping every time he had them, though he'd never shown any interesting camping or basically any outdoor activity before. Then, once he got to the camping spot, he would have them call me crying to drive out to wherever they were and get them, knowing full well there was no way I could do it. He probably wouldn't have let them leave even if I had. He would force them to watch scary movies like I Know What You Did Last Summer, and then they would have nightmares for weeks (remember they were 9, 6, and 2 at the time). I don't know if he was just trying to get even with me, or if he was that clueless about parenting. It was all so bizarre. The list goes on and on; he was every bit as horrible to the kids as he was to me. Kevin was always quick to point out this was divorce, and I was the one who wanted it. I was on the verge of a nervous breakdown; we had to get out of there.

## DOCHOLLYWOOD007

Even after everything that had already happened, I can still remember thinking…. "Okay God, I know I have *plenty* of reasons to divorce him, but I need to know I am doing the right thing. I need to know that he really is never going to change." And there it was, just like that, all the evidence I needed!

My computer was running slow, so my sister was attempting to clean off the hard drive. Apparently there are temporary folders that your hard drive stores, who knew? As she went along, she stumbled across some temporary folders that had somehow automatically saved. There were 8 of them to be exact, from the previous year. They were all full of pages from a website called fling.com; apparently, my husband was a member.

For those of you who don't know, fling.com is like a Myspace for sex. There he was! We stumbled upon his page, under the code name

"*DocHollywood007.*" There were pages and pages of emails he'd sent to other women, hotel reservations, etc. Guess he really wasn't on call all of those nights? The sad thing was, I can remember several times I kept the kids out of the house so he could sleep, or he was unable to attend their ball games because he was "*sleeping.*" Turns out, he had reservations on those nights. Who calls themselves Doc Hollywood 007 anyway? What a *douche canoe*!!!

I found out later he was also on many other dating websites. Either he was really good at sneaking around, or I was really dumb and naïve (you're not the only one going with the latter). Either way, it really didn't matter at that point. I was just *relieved* to be getting out of the situation.

When you're a nurse, your unit is like your family. We tend to tell each other EVERYTHING! Especially in a large city, when none of us even live in the same area; your secrets are pretty safe. After several of the nurses

I worked with found out about husband's double life, they began searching for him. There he was *again*, under the name "*HOT4U2NITE*." So creative, I mean really, how does he come up with this stuff? Since DOCHOLLYWOOD007 was no longer available, they began messaging him (Hot4u2nite) trying to meet up. Their plan was to tie him to the bed naked and walk out. It would've been hilarious, just like a scene from a movie; only apparently, he was checking my voicemail and overhearing a message, he realized what was happening. Who knew you needed a password on your voicemail?

## *AN END IN SIGHT*

Christmas was approaching, and our 60-day waiting period was up. We had a meeting scheduled with our attorneys to get everything settled. Kevin was trying to delay it, stating his attorney would be gone on vacation. This would delay us being able to move over Christmas break, which was what I *desperately* wanted. I knew what he was up to, so when Kevin showed up the day before our scheduled meeting, I told him he WOULD be at that meeting, and we would reach an agreement allowing me and the kids to move back home; or, I would go to the medical board and notify them of all his illegal behaviors (prostitution, excessive drinking, writing prescriptions for himself and his friends, etc.). He was livid and got in my face screaming and cussing. I had never in my life seen him so angry, he was completely out of control. My sister was so scared she called the police and he left. The next day my attorney received a letter from his, stating I was blackmailing him and they were going to press charges. Say what? Me blackmail? Just stating the facts baby, it worked. He was at the meeting, and we reached an agreement, which allowed us to move out of Harris County.

I wouldn't say I came out with *everything* I wanted. I probably would have come out better in court, but I was desperate to move and have some guidelines to follow. My attorney never had temporary orders set, so I hadn't been receiving any child support or help with bills for the past 6 months. I guess you get what you pay for, although it did end up costing $14,000 in the end. I don't understand why we hadn't gone for a little help with bills at the very least. I had gotten to the point where I hadn't been able to even make the last couple of house payments. My salary could only go so far, and we had too many bills for me to possibly cover them all without a little help.

We basically did everything by the book. We split the debt, he got his student loans, which were a large amount (probably why he could afford a ski trip), and I got more of the credit card debt. Nobody wanted the house; although, he was supposed to catch up the payments and put it on the market, he never did. Visitation was standard; he would get them every other weekend. I stupidly agreed to drive them to him once a month (4 hours each way). By the way, don't EVER do that. Agree to as little driving as possible. HUGE mistake!  Best of all, the kids and I got to *move*!! We signed the papers, and my attorney and I were meeting at the courthouse at 8AM the following morning.

I went home and celebrated with my mom and sister; it was over. Finally, FREE AT LAST!! I could breathe. For the first time in months, I could breathe. A 1,000 lb. weight had been lifted off my shoulders. We had rules, structure, and child support. My personal hell was almost over. I didn't want to wait another minute.

Keeping in the theme of my life in Houston, my washing machine had broken earlier during the week, and I hadn't bothered to get it fixed in the hope that we were soon moving.  My mom left and went home shortly after the meeting, leaving, my sister, me, and the kids at home. That night, as we got ready for bed, the stomach virus came to visit all three kids simultaneously. Every 15-30 minutes someone was puking, bright pink, chunky vomit. It. Was. Everywhere. No one was able to make it to a toilet, sink, trashcan, or any place that may have made it easier to clean. It was *horrid*, like a scene from a movie. At that point, what could I do? All we could do …was lie on the floor and laugh. Remember? My washing machine was broken. By the end of the night, we were all sleeping on towels. I had rinsed and bagged up 5 trash bags FULL of laundry to take to the Laundromat the following morning. After I met my attorney at the courthouse, of course. No way was I letting ANYTHING detour me from getting my divorce finalized. So there I was at 8 am sharp, and that was it. It was official; the nightmare had ended, kind of. On the way home, I got pulled over by a police officer (luckily got off with a warning) for running a stop sign; I guess I didn't even see it amidst all the excitement! As soon as I got home, I headed to the Laundromat with 3 sick kids. What a great celebration to my divorce being final!!! Such is life!

Christmas passed, and we were getting ready for the big move. Kevin was insistent on getting everything in the house.  I had only asked for the bedroom furniture, computer, and of course whatever he didn't want.  I think by the end of it he had 2 refrigerators, 3 microwaves, and whatever else he could think of to claim.  The kids were upset about everything he was trying to take; they just didn't understand.  We often found ourselves listening to that George Strait song *"Just Give It Away."*  Truly, there wasn't anything in that house worth fighting over.  And while he was at it, keep it and shove it where the sun doesn't shine for all I care.  We would sing and dance to that song while we were packing our things. It may seem kind of corny, I know, but it added the humor we needed to get through.

Kevin had the kids beginning on the 28th and he decided to take the girls skiing.  I guess he had saved a lot of money not paying any bills for 6 months!  Where they went skiing I'm still not sure.  The only information I was given about it was a text message saying, "I'm taking the kids skiing for vacation, maybe you can take them to

Big Rocks (a local hangout at the river in the small town we were from)." He refused to tell me anything else. Needless to say, it was the *longest* week of my life. He left my son with me, but I had no clue where my girls were, where they were staying, or whom they were even with. I guess one would assume parents could be mature and respectful enough to give this info to the other parent; however, there is no way to enforce it. It was his week, and I had no control over it. All I could do was pray they made it back in one piece, unscathed. We spent the week moving, and finally a fresh start!

## *ATTORNEYS: WHAT YOU NEED TO KNOW*

I honestly do not have anything to positive to say in regards to attorneys. I think the majority of them are out to get your money and are in no rush to settle your case.

1.     You should be able to get a consultation for free. Do not pay anyone a retainer fee until you

have met with him or her and they have reviewed your case.

2.     Talk to previous clients, they should be able to get you references.  You can also call the county clerk's office and ask for recommendations on whom to use.

3.     Divorce, at least in the state of Texas, is pretty black and white.  Anyone promising you the moon may not be being very truthful.  It is what it is.  Everything is split 50/50 from what you have in the bank, investments, and debt.

4.     Custody is usually joint with the mother being the custodial parent.  Joint custody is when the dad gets the child every 1st, 3rd, and 5th weekend and one night during the week.  A lot of fathers go for shared-custody, which means you split the kids every other week and they don't pay child support.  What you have to ask yourself is, "Is he dependable?"  My ex lied about working all of the time and he never helped me, so I knew that would never work.  An arrangement like that

would have left me not only parenting by myself, but also without any financial assistance. My advice is to always agree to the least amount of visitation on paper. It may sound mean, but you don't have to go strictly by the divorce decree and you can always let him see them more.

5.      Make sure your child support and health insurance is set up through the attorney general's office, through the state and not through your county. It will eliminate arguing with your ex over money, and should they ever get behind on their child support, they will provide you with legal assistance. If your ex changes jobs, they will also track down their new place of employment and reestablish payment. If they are supposed to reimburse you for insurance, there has to be a set dollar amount in the decree in order for it to be enforced.

6.      Remember, anything you put in the decree applies to both of you. For example, should the decree read that a member of the opposite sex not be allowed over past 9 pm or to stay the night, it

applies to both of you. You may think that's fine, but while you have no plans of ever letting a man stay over, things may change in the future.

7. Alimony in the state of Texas is near impossible. You have to have been married a minimum of 10 years with no means to support yourself. Even at that, it is usually only for a limited amount of time.

# HE SAYS: WHAT IT REALLY MEANS

*He says: I'm going out for ice cream*

*What it really means: I'm going to call or "see" my girlfriend.*

Crazy, I know. Ice cream is one of America's favorite past times, right? Innocent enough, one would think. Six months to a year after the hooker incident, Kevin started going out for ice cream in the evening to the local Marble Slab. I never really thought much about it. He usually returned home still eating on it. After word had gotten out at the hospital were I was working, one of my coworkers asked if he always went out for ice cream. At first, the question struck me as odd, and I sat there and thought about it. He had been going out for ice cream for the past year at least 4-5 times per week. Her ex-husband was also a physician / alcoholic/ prescription drug addict/ sex addict, and that was how he had managed to find the time to call his girlfriends (paid or unpaid)! Who would have thought? Something as simple as ice cream could be used for something so dirty.

*He says: I have to work late. I left something at the office. I have to go by the store.*

*What it really means: Same. Same. Same. Lies. Lies. Lies. He is with his girlfriend, a hooker, or someone other than you.*

This is not to say just because your husband works late he's cheating. These are changes in patterns of behavior, a change in hours, or routine. Something is off. Deep down you probably know it seems weird but you're either too exhausted or too busy to worry about it, or care. Maybe you're tired of never being able to catch him even though you know something is off. Maybe he calls in sick to work but doesn't even tell you he is sick. And you're a nurse? Either way, here are your red flags. Open your eyes, take a good luck, and save yourself some time.

*He says: Those aren't mine, I was holding them for a friend. My friend didn't have any money and I had to pay. They moved the date of the test.*

*What it really means: He's hiding something. He can't take responsibility for his actions. Nothing ever adds up and it is never going to.*

Have you ever found pills, drugs, or porn? Oh wait, your husband was stashing it for his friend too? His friend didn't want his wife to find it, but your husband wasn't worried? You would know it was not his right? You're cool and understanding. He's a great guy, always bailing everyone else out. All these charges to your debit card, maybe a credit card you didn't know he had? It's exhausting. It never adds up. He never follows through with anything. He never admits to anything until you can prove it. Please, ain't nobody got time for playing detective all the time.

*He says: I have a room reserved for you and your sister at the fat farm…don't keep them waiting!*

*What it really means: I can't believe you left me and I'm going to hurt you in any way possible.*

This is by far one of my favorite text messages I ever received. The moment it came through, my sister and I literally lay on the floor laughing our asses off. First off, not that there's anything wrong with being overweight, but I have always worked out and tried to take care of myself. The point is, it doesn't matter if you're overweight or not. Men know weight is something we all worry and obsess about, and it's one area that is going to hurt us whether we have some extra pounds on us or not. I do have to admit I think it was a very original, somewhat hilarious text message. Seriously though, *grow up*! I never sent anything about how big his nose was, how hairy his legs were, or how disgusting his white, moly skin was. I mean you can always lose weight, but you can't fix ugly, or stupid for that matter! How does that saying go?  Those that live in glass houses shouldn't throw stones.

*He says: You'll never find someone who will want you with 3 kids.  They might sleep with you, but they'll never want a relationship with you.*

*What it really means: I can't stand the thought of you being with someone else.  I know I've messed up, maybe if I destroy your self-esteem then you won't ever meet anyone.*

First off, does he not have three kids too?  I thought we had them together?  Why would someone date him with three kids and not me?  Give me a break.  The simple truth is, I haven't met a guy since my divorce that cared I had kids.  If he does care, he's not worth dating anyways!  The thing is, we all get to an age that everyone you know has children.  People expect it.  There are great men out there who will love your kids as much as they love you; because, your kids are part of you.  Sure, you can find plenty of people to sleep with you, married or unmarried, but there are also plenty that want a real relationship with you. Do not listen. Do not be afraid. He is an idiot.

*He says: You were such a terrible wife and I was so unhappy. That's the reason I drank and cheated.*

*What it really means: I can't take responsibility for my actions so I am going to place the blame wherever I can.*

Really? I was a terrible wife. What kind of husband do you think you were? What did I get out of the relationship? I worked full time, took care of three kids by myself, paid all the bills, took care of the house, and did all the yard work. You want to talk about needing some attention? How about giving me a little help? Instead of drinking and having an affair, I was too busy *busting my ass*! I don't know why men don't realize it's a two-way street. You want me to look good, bring home a paycheck, take care of everything with the kids and house, and then you want to complain whenever you aren't getting enough attention. And blame your cheating and drinking on me? I don't even think so. Exactly what is it you think I got out of that relationship (other than you doing your best to give me an STD, which is not exactly what I had in mind)?

# THE AFTERMATH

## _THE HOUSE THAT BUILT ME_

They say you can't go home again. Well hello Glendale, we're back! We moved in with my parents. I was 28 years old, and my children and I were living with Nanny and Pop. Upstairs there are 3 bedrooms, a bathroom, and a living area. I wanted it to be as normal as possible for my kids, so I took the living area and gave each of the kids their own room. Who needs a closet anyways?

My parents were in the process of building a house right down the street on some land they already owned. The plan was we would stay in their house, which is the one I actually grew up in, and I would rent it from them once they moved. It took 8 long months for them to finish their new home. I love my parents, I'm fortunate enough to have the type of family you WANT to be around. Difficult would be the only word to describe moving back in with mom and dad, for them, and for me. There was no space and no privacy, but you do what you have to do. I didn't have a lot of options, but this was the best option of them.  It allowed me time to get back on my feet and save some money.  For that, I am eternally grateful.  I don't know how I would've managed everything if it weren't for my mom and dad.  My parents are *seriously* the best. I will forever be grateful for their generosity and grace.

We got the kids all settled in their new schools. My daughters were in 4th and 1st grade, beginning right after Christmas Break.  We made a point of having them meet some kids prior to their first day.   Another bonus of a small town, we pretty much knew everyone and who they belonged to.

Finding childcare was an entire issue in itself. There were no churches or larger daycare centers like we had become accustomed to in Lubbock and Houston.  There were two small daycare centers, which I visited and then considered welfare because I would not be able to work and leave my sweet, baby boy in that filth.  Seriously, no exaggerations here.  Not only was it disgusting, the staff wasn't qualified to care for animals, much less children – that brought my options to in-home daycares.

The problem with in-home daycares is they are limited in the number of children they can take under a certain age, meaning no more than 6. Finally, we found a sweet older lady with an opening.  Her house was clean, and she was trustworthy.  She had good references, we knew other people who left their children there, and frankly she was our last option if I was going to work.

It was hard moving back to the small town my ex-husband and I had both grown up in. Knowing everyone was talking about why we had gotten divorced was a hard one to swallow. After all, if you don't know what's happening in your own life, someone in a small town can surely tell you!  Of course, half the town had seen this coming from the day we said I DO.  It was humiliating, but it was all a truth I had to face.  I just had to put on my big girl panties, hold my head up high, and move forward with my life.

I can remember being at the local Dairy Queen with my sister, yes the fact we have a Dairy Queen should say a lot. We had taken the kids for ice cream after their first day of school. There were several groups of women, all whispering and staring at us, it was hard to miss. As much as I wanted to walk over and give them a piece of my mind, I refrained. At this point, I didn't want to bite off more than I could chew. I had enough on my plate as it was. Truth be told, their opinions didn't matter anyway. Luckily, it got easier as time went on, and the news slowly died down. There lies another bonus of a small town; it doesn't take long for the talk to move on to someone else. So hold tight, this too shall pass.

The harassment from Kevin continued. It was *exhausting.* I was tired, worn down, and fed up. Something had to give. My mom decided she was going to give me a break and deal with him, hoping to mend fences. No matter what we did, it was wrong. We picked the wrong babysitter (like there was another option, but that would require being involved to know that), we hadn't told him enough information about the kids, he didn't agree with the doctor's diagnosis if the kids were sick, etc. You name it, we had done it wrong, said it wrong, and were all around wrong. It got so bad, my mom wasn't able to eat or sleep. He was constantly emailing or calling her, multiple times a day, complaining or bashing me. Kevin would use anything he could come up with to try and make me look bad. Let's be honest here, compared to what you've done, sweetheart, I look like an angel. Sorry I don't abuse drugs and alcohol, sleep with hookers, or abuse women and children.

Poor Nanny finally had to go to the doctor and get on anti-anxiety medication. She had become a nervous wreck. Eventually, truly about a month later, it all came to a head when he wanted to switch weekends, and we already had plans, leaving us unable to switch. Kevin flipped his lid on her, called her a *"lying bitch,"* told her he would no longer deal with her, and would only deal with me. Yeah, me!!! What a *little prick*, how dare you call my mother names? My family was good to that asshole for 10 years. They treated him like their own child, and that's how you want to play? After all the hookers, alcohol, and drugs, all he had put us through. *Unbelievable.*

I finally found the best way to deal with Kevin was to involve him in as little as possible. It was sad, I really tried to keep him involved even after all he had done, but he was barking up the wrong tree. He made it impossible to communicate with him or include him in any decision. We had to limit all communication and try to cut as many ties as possible. Two words: narcissistic sociopath. We had no other options. We began only notifying him of what we were *legally* obligated to. Maybe that's wrong, but he was too much to deal with, and my kids were getting the short end of the stick. We quit sending their prescriptions, because they wouldn't get returned or given, and would just begin them again once they got home. Being a doctor, you would think he of all people would realize the importance of completing antibiotics. Nope, just give them a little Tylenol and TLC that will fix it! Sure it will. We couldn't pack anything to go with them that mattered if it returned at all, because it just simply wouldn't.

I was working at a surgery center 30 minutes away. I couldn't find a labor and delivery job that didn't require weekends, and honestly it would never compare to Women's. I needed a career change that didn't involve weekends or holidays. I had only done Labor and Delivery for the past 7 years; it was time to do something new. I knew trying to manage working weekends and driving the kids to Houston once a month would only add more stress. So, I was on to a new chapter. I was newly divorced, had a new place to live, new job, new field, new schools. I guess you could say 2008 was a year of *new beginnings*!

Have you ever felt like God puts certain people in your life for a reason? He knew I needed support, and that's exactly what he gave me. I worked with the most wonderful group of encouraging, Christian women. People I could talk to, confide in, and vent my frustrations to. Several of us were going through difficult times during the period of time I worked there. Free support groups are my favorite! I was battling a lot during that time, obviously. Newly divorced, moving back to the small town I'd grown up in, dealing with a *psychotic* ex-husband.... you know, the usual. These girls really saw me through to the other side of it.

When I left Houston, the saddest part was leaving my friends. They were my other family. I didn't think I would ever be able to find friends like that again. Here they were though, my girls. The latest escapades of my crazy ex had become a joke between all of us girls and the surgeons.

Every week when someone new came in they asked the same question. What's the latest? Any crazy texts? How *crazy* was the kids' visit? It was always so insane that no one could help but to ask about it!

The funniest thing to me about that time was Kevin always sent psychotic text messages with different scriptures stating I was going to hell for divorcing him, how happy he was without me, how he hoped I could find the same kind of happiness one day too, and the best was how he'd met the love of his life and how wonderful she was (funny, they're no longer together). At this point, we were down to less than 10 messages a day, and he was given a time restriction in which I would not respond. Nothing after 10 pm or before 7 am.

After about a year of working at the surgery center, my boss, who had also become one of my closest friends, went through a divorce. Her husband had a meth addiction, 3 kids, and she could no longer live with the lying and sneaking around either.  Reading the constant emails and text messages, and all the harassment, was just like going through it with Kevin.  Crazy, right? Not really.  Three words: addict, narcissist, sociopath.  It's like they have a book of what to say, how to try and take no responsibility for their actions, and turn it ALL around on you at the same time. They were two peas in a pod.  I am so thankful for that job and those women.  I can't imagine what it would've been like to not have their support, as well as my families.

## CONSIDER THE CONSEQUENCES

One big mistake I made in my divorce was agreeing to drive the kids to Houston the first weekend of every month.  Kevin would be responsible for getting them on the 3rd and 5th weekends.  I'm sure this will shock you— he rarely showed up to get them on his weekends to drive and typically only saw them on the weekends I drove.  I agreed to drive once a month, mainly because that was the only way he would agree to us moving, and I was going to miss all of my friends terribly. I thought it would be a good opportunity to see them. FYI the normal arrangement for a parent living over 100 miles is to meet halfway, once a month. Thanks to my *awesome* attorney, I was unaware of that.

So, every month I drove the kids to Houston, a good 4.5 hours away from where we lived. I would stay the weekend with a friend and we would go out the entire weekend. It was great to see everybody and catch up, although the drive home with three kids (not feeling quite up to par from the night before) was *long* and got *old* really fast!! I loved my friends, but once I had my own life in Glendale, I came to dread that drive.

On the weekends I drove, Kevin would usually try to negotiate me driving the kids a 2nd weekend or trading weekends before he would give them back to me. I wasn't going to drive them two weekends in one month when he could rarely make it down for one. I did try to trade when possible but wasn't always able to accommodate due to other commitments.

When Kevin didn't get his way, he exploded. I'm not sure that is even a strong enough word. He would fly off the handle, half-cocked. He wouldn't give the kids back until 6:00 pm, they still needed to get their stuff together, AND he hadn't fed them dinner, putting us home at 11:00 pm, at the earliest, on a school night. He would say, "kids are resilient; they can just sleep in the car" (After all, he is a doctor, I'm sure he was right). Kevin would call me every name in the book and sometimes threaten to not give the kids back. He would *refuse* to open the gate to his apartment, and I would once again have to wait for someone to leave so I could get in. It was a *beating,* to say the least. It wasn't fair to my kids, and, it wasn't fair to me. It was bad enough they had been through a divorce, but worse that he looked for ways to punish them just to get at me.

I was the only one doing any driving, and Kevin used it as an opportunity to try and manipulate things. You just can't give someone with that

kind of selfish, immoral character ANY control.
They will seize any opportunity possible to use it
against you. We had to limit his control in every
situation possible and only tell him about
circumstances were obligated to. I didn't ask him
questions and I didn't provide any information
that wasn't absolutely necessary. I tried to
answer any questions as simply as possible and
limit discussions strictly to his weekends with the
kids and what activities they had.

I had driven the kids down to Houston the first
weekend of May. To our surprise, he had a
female "friend" in for the weekend. Her name
was Hope, or maybe it was Faith? I really can't
remember. As soon as I picked the kids up, they
*raved* about how wonderful she was and how
they thought she was going to be their new step
mom. As I later found out, he met her on
fling.com. Of course they loved her! Who
wouldn't? He didn't get the kids the 3rd or 5th
weekends; I believe he said he was working??
That's funny in itself; wouldn't you know before

Thursday night if you were working that weekend? Hmm, guess I'm too stupid to figure that one out! When you gotta work, you gotta work (although I feel like our idea of work may differ a little).

I drove the kids down the first weekend in June, where they were introduced to his girlfriend Jenna. They thought she was okay, but she was no Hope. Of course she wasn't, Hope was from fling.com, and Jenna was a nurse he worked with at the hospital. Definitely no comparison there!

Two weeks later, Kevin actually came to Glendale to see the kids. He took them to a waterpark up in the metroplex, where he introduced them to a girl named Kaylee. Apparently, he met her on a Christian dating website. Fabulous! Three different women, three weekends in a row. Stability is key. The kids asked about Jenna and were told they had broken up. Funny though, she was back in the picture the next time he got them. He's a snake in the grass, couldn't trust him farther than you could throw him.  Shockingly, nothing had changed.  Once a cheater, always a cheater; if they'll cheat with you, they'll cheat on you!

# PSYCHOLOGICAL WARFARE

*Narcissist:* noun 1. A person who is overly self-involved, and often vain and selfish. 2. One with an inflated sense of their own importance, a deep need for admiration, and a lack of empathy for others. Sometimes parent –child relationships or genetics can result in the narcissistic personality.

*Sociopath:* Anti-personality Disorder. A mental condition in which a person has a long-term pattern of manipulating, exploiting, or violating the rights of others. It is usually a result from complex interaction of genetic and environmental factors (child abuse, alcoholic parents). Sociopathy is more common in men than women.

*Psychoanalysis:* A person who suffers from narcissism, deriving erotic gratification from the admiration of his or her own physical or mental attributes. They often come across as conceited or boastful. This sense of entitlement leaves them angry and impatient when they don't get what they feel they deserve. To feel better, they react with rage or belittle the other person. A narcissist often suffers from a fragile, low self-esteem in which they are trying to protect and hide their real insecurities. Combine the narcissist with the sociopath? You get my ex-husband. A true piece of work, and extremely difficult to deal with.

One conclusion I've come to is that every narcissist basically has the same story. You could literally take 100 women that were once married to a narcissist and listen to them exchange a different version of the same story over and over. The manipulation, the blame, the lies, nothing is ever their fault. They have an *excuse* for everything. Not only is it not their fault, it's probably yours. You are to blame; you don't give them enough attention, you don't touch them enough, you don't look good enough, and you don't keep the house clean enough. They are always the victim. If you would have been a better wife, a better lover, a better companion, they wouldn't have been forced to get attention elsewhere.

Narcissists are all about the show, and they are usually very successful. After all, they are better than the rest of us, right? This is why they are often people in positions of power such as CEO's, attorneys, doctors, etc. They like to be the center of attention and recognized for their accomplishments. Combine a sociopath with a narcissist, and you have someone willing to do whatever it takes to be on top. This is called the narcissistic sociopath. They are master manipulators, which is exactly why you don't see it coming. They don't care who they hurt, who they humiliate, or whom they step on along the way. They are charming, and often make you feel special. Yet, if you pay close attention, it doesn't take long to realize these are just words. Their words never match their actions; they're *completely* superficial. They literally don't mean most of what they say and you are left with a bunch of empty promises. They have an excuse for everything.  You will NEVER get an apology – unless they are caught red handed, of course. Even at that, you probably did something to cause it.

I can remember the dreaded feeling I would get in the pit of my stomach when leaving work. What condition would Kevin be in when I got home?  Would he be drunk?  Would the sitter still be there or would my children be alone with him? This was when his drinking was at an all-time high.  I would come home, and he would be falling down drunk, unable to hold an intelligent conversation, and unable to care for the children. He was definitely in no condition to drive or even change a diaper for that matter. I would confront him, and he would deny it.  I would search the house, the garage, and the trashcans until I found whatever his pleasure was that night.  Beer, wine, crown royal, not to mention his poly pharmacy.  I would line it up on the counter, and then he *might* admit to it, if I was lucky.  For anyone that's ever lived with an alcoholic, the smell of mouthwash combined with alcohol is *unmistakable*. To this day it brings back a flood of memories. There isn't a smell quite like it.

They're impulsive and risky. Immediate gratification is the motto they live by. This is why they often turn to alcohol, drugs, and women. They need to feel good immediately. When they want something, they want it right then. They can't wait until they've earned something or worked for it. When we were in college, Kevin decided we needed to take a vacation to Europe. We didn't have the money, but that was what he thought he needed. We packed up the baby and blew all of our grant money. That money should've been for tuition, daycare, bills, etc. Europe is the type of trip you take when you graduate from college and you have REAL jobs. He also decided he needed a motorcycle, a big screen TV, a new car, etc. If he wanted it, he got it. Never mind the fact my parents were paying our rent to make it easier for both of us to go to school.

The sad reality is, we as human beings want to see the good in people. None of us are perfect, we all screw up, and we all make mistakes. The *difference* is the rest of us feel remorse. We go out of our way to NOT hurt people. We want to forgive people, and that's what we are called to do. Forgiveness however, does not mean we are doormats. It doesn't mean we have to continually get trampled all over. We can't always fix people; some people won't change no matter how hard you try. This makes us a target. We are vulnerable and caring. We let our guard down way to easily. We are easily manipulated and naïve. We can't be targets and we have to recognize these red flags.

How to deal with a narcissistic sociopath:

1.    *Run the other direction.* This is not a warning. Cut all strings and get the hell out of there. Things will not change. You will not fix him. You are the next victim.

2.    *Pick your battles.* Have you heard the saying, "it's like arguing with a brick wall?" This was developed because of the narcissistic sociopath. You will not win, they are right, you are wrong, and it's all your fault. Don't waste your time, you will be frustrated, angry, and the results will not change.

3.    *Never let them see you cry.* This is what they thrive off of. They want to know they hurt you, this means they've won. Worse yet, it's a guarantee they will do it again. Once they know your vulnerabilities they will use them against you, to manipulate you. To get what they want.

4.    *Do not react.* No matter how mad you are or how bad you want to, don't do it. It won't change anything. It only reinforces they know how to push your buttons. Once again, they win. You will not prove a point to them. You will not show them the light. They will only flip it around on you and make you feel as though you are the crazy one. They will not be able to deal with you when you are so out of control. They will use

this opportunity to show their loved ones how crazy you truly are. Once again, they win.

5.    *Do not share any plans ahead of time*. Tell them the bare minimum, only what's necessary. They will take every opportunity and step to ruin any plans. Therefore, always have a backup. For example, if you're taking a trip with a new love interest and plan on leaving the kids with your ex, have a backup. It is a guarantee they will have something come up and will be unable to keep the kids; therefore, your trip is ruined. Do not give them that control. Always have an option 2 or 3. Do not rely on them for anything.

6.    *They want control and will do anything to have it*. Do not give them any extra power. Do not let them give you money or gifts. If they are buying something for the children make it clear that it is for their child, it has nothing to do with you. Do not ask them for help. This is another opportunity for them to have control. Unfortunately, you married a narcissistic sociopath, you don't get to have that kind of

relationship. These are not normal people. You cannot trust them. They do not care about anyone but themselves, their wants, and their needs.

7.    *Document, Document, Document.* If it isn't written down, it didn't happen. Try communicating about anything big by email or text. Keep a journal. These are admissible in court should you ever need it in the future and they know it. Should you have a disagreement or he tries to say y'all agreed upon something else, you can resort to your conversation. You have proof it happened. They cannot lie about what you said or they said. Protect yourself first.

# LET YOUR INNER LIONESS OUT

Welcome to the heavy stuff. This is probably the *hardest* part. I think we work ourselves up into thinking we are going to traumatize our children for life. Divorce is the end all. Two words; social outcast. Our secret is going to be out of the closet! We are dysfunctional. We don't have it all together. We are a *hot mess*, trying to put on the façade of a mother who has it all together. We had the beautiful house, beautiful family, great job, perfect marriage, and to top it off, we found time to exercise and look good. Now the truth is going to come out, it was all a lie.

We have to ask ourselves what's better, growing up in a healthy home or a dysfunctional home? That is the real question. We have all these crazy thoughts and justifications of why we should stay – it's better for our children, divorce can screw kids up for life, etc. By golly, we are going to break the cycle! However, the real cycle is broken when we don't marry the asshole to begin with.

We need to wake up and educate our daughters about why it is important to wait until they are emotionally ready to enter into a sexual relationship, how important it is to choose a partner that values and respects you, and how to recognize the signs of a narcissist. Teach them how to love and respect themselves enough that they will settle for nothing less. It would be nice if we all waited until we were married, but that's not reality. So, instead of pretending our daughters are above premarital sex, let's teach them how to practice safe sex. We don't have to make it easy or give them permission, but we can ensure that if they are going to make that choice, they will protect themselves.

We have to ask ourselves if we are staying for our kids or because of our own fear. Fear of the unknown, fear of doing it alone, fear of loneliness and not being able to succeed, or fear of failure. Put your fears aside, man up, and do what is best for your children.  Be the example.  Show them how to be strong, courageous, and determined. Rant over.

My ex-husband grew up in a VERY dysfunctional family.  His dad had infidelity issues from the time Kevin was young; his parents slept in separate rooms for the last 10 years of their marriage.  My ex actually found videos of his dad with prostitutes in hotel rooms when he was in junior high.  Kevin's infidelity was a learned behavior. My point is not to bash Kevin's family or air their laundry.  The point is he *never* saw what normal was.  He didn't learn a husband should respect and honor his wife. Kevin missed out on seeing the love and respect a couple should have for one another.  Point being, he never grew up seeing a *normal* relationship because his parents were trying to shelter him from going through a divorce as a child.  He has issues to say the least, as you're well aware by this point, some genetic – others environmental.

I refuse to believe keeping your children in a dysfunctional home helps them in anyway. We all have experiences in life that guide the decisions we make... this being one for me. It takes two people to make a marriage work. One person can't do it alone. You can't make someone WANT to be with you or treat you right. You can't do it alone, and I don't believe God wants us to. He doesn't want you to be a *doormat* for someone to walk all over. Husbands and wives should respect each other and put the needs of one another before their own. That's how I believe a marriage should work. That's the example I want to set for my children. A family that prays together stays together. God has to be first, then your marriage, children, family, etc.

Now how do you tell the kids? How much should they know? Sure, I think the child's age during the divorce will highly dictate how much you tell them. Most importantly, I think it's important they have a *reason* for the divorce. They need to know it is not their fault. They didn't do anything wrong. I'm not saying to give them the entire reason. They don't need to know more than they can handle. They definitely don't need all the dirty, scanty details. The children should NOT have to choose sides.

We told our kids we were getting divorced because their daddy had a drinking problem. Number one, I wasn't taking the blame for it. Number two, they had seen this and already knew it was a problem. We didn't tell them details, and we certainly didn't tell them about all of the cheating. They had a reason though, and they knew it had nothing to do with them. It wasn't their fault. I'm not saying it was easy. Sure, it was hard on them at first, but over time they began to realize this was just the way things were. It wasn't hard on them because they wanted us together. It was hard on them because it was changing their lives, their routines. They didn't get to sleep in their own beds every night. They didn't get a say in where they slept. They were losing what little control they felt like they had over their own lives, and that's a hard adjustment for anyone.  As if a divorce isn't hard enough for everyone involved, Kevin didn't make it any easier either.  If Kevin thought it would get to me or give him some control, he *seized* the opportunity, regardless of how he hurt his children.

The kids should *always* come first— sometimes that's easier said than done, however.  As much as I hated my ex-husband, I have always tried to approach every decision regarding the children by saying to myself, "what is in my kids' best interest?"  I am by no means a saint, and there are plenty of times I let my anger and resentment cloud my judgment.  As much as I would like to pretend I am perfect and above it, I am just as much of a hot mess as the next guy. When it comes to a decision regarding the children, however, like switching weekends, days, or holidays, I try to think of what they will have to miss if I switch, and what is best for them without screwing up my schedule or plans too much. Basically, it has to work best for all involved.

Sometimes we have to *compromise*, even though we don't want to. Other times, we don't. We have to put our foot down and go with what is best for us or for our children. For the most part, I think I do pretty well with that. It is hard though. I think the main thing is to keep your eye on the prize...*helping* your kids grow up to be strong, caring, confident, great people. That is the goal, and frankly, nothing else really makes a rat's ass. Regardless of how much you hate your ex, they need to be some part of your kids' lives. I would never want my children to feel like their dad abandoned them or didn't love them, no matter how much I hate him. That would only hurt my kids and give them obstacles to overcome in the future.

Both of my daughters used to call around bedtime every night they were with their dad, crying for me to come and pick them up. It didn't matter where he had taken them or what they were doing, it was constant in the beginning. If they were camping several hours away, he would tell them they could go home if I would come pick them up (yeah right, like he would've allowed that) or they could be right down the street. I wanted to go pick my babies up more than anything, but I knew if I did, they would never get used to staying with him, and they would never quit calling me to come and get them. Plus, that also was a way for him to control me, to ruin any plans I had, and to always keep me on edge. If he knew he could use them to control me, he would never stop. He would continue to use and hurt them to make me feel bad, trying to continue making his point that this was what divorce is.

Instead, I reassured them I loved them; that their dad loved them, and they would get to come home very soon. I told them I couldn't come and get them because it was their dad's time with them and he wanted to see them (that was not the easiest thing to explain when he was intentionally trying to upset them to hurt me). I did it anyways. That's my job, reassurance, instilling confidence, and adjustment. Motherhood isn't always easy, and it often tests us more than we would like to admit. It was difficult for me and for them, and they continued calling, wanting to come home for about a year. It got better and they learned how to deal with it. They learned to quit fighting it, along with some other valuable lessons. They learned how to adjust to difficult situations, how to *stand up* for themselves, and how to stand on their own two feet. We may not like our circumstances and we may not be able to change them, but we do have to learn how to make the best out of them.

Don't you just hate when people turn out to be complete hypocrites? It's beyond frustrating! Kevin became quite the health nut after we split up. Can you believe it? He never drank or abused prescription drugs again. It was a Christmas *miracle*! It's hard to believe, I'm sure, after reading about the sex, drugs, and alcohol.

He worked out all the time and only ate limited portions. He was SO healthy. He was an iron man. Of course like most addicts, everything he does is to the extreme, obsessive even.

Since Kevin became SO awesome and healthy, he decided to limit the amount of food my kids ate too. They weren't allowed to have snacks, sometimes they didn't get fed lunch or dinner, or when they did, it was really late. They weren't growing, right? They don't know when they're hungry. Kevin could survive on an apple all day (yet he wasn't on anything) so they ought to be able to as well. This was difficult to accept for me. I would see him and feel like a beast in the wild. It took all the restraint I had to keep from picking up the nearest chair and *slamming* it over his head. FEED MY CHILDREN, be a parent, and try to be a little normal. How dare he hurt my babies? We are their protectors and their providers. Just as I do in any distressing situation, I tried to find the positive. Seriously, what else could I do?

After picking my kids up in Houston one weekend, the girls proceeded to tell me about how Saturday they were FINALLY given an apple for breakfast, and then they didn't get lunch until 4:00pm. Their dad and his girlfriend had finally taken them to Pei Wei. By that point, they were starving, so naturally they went to the bathroom, stuffed a bunch of fortune cookies in their purses on the way in, and sat in there and ate them. The next morning it was 10:00 am and they couldn't get their dad or his girlfriend to wake up and fix breakfast. So, they snuck in a bedroom and finished off the rest of the fortune cookies. They then added, "We didn't give any to our little brother because we thought he might tell our dad," poor baby boy, he just had to go hungry! While a little bit *heartbroken* at the story, I was laughing so hard at their account of the weekend and how proud of themselves they were. What can I say, he was teaching my kids to become resourceful!

I've always heard to never bad mouth your ex to your children. They will figure it out on their own, and it will only hurt them and push them away if you do. This is one thing I have always abided by and TRULY believe is important. I do not say anything about him; however, I do occasionally validate their feelings when they tell me how weird he is, or what a jerk they think he is. All I say is, *"I agree with you completely"* or *"hmm...that is weird"*. I think it's important for them to be able to express how they feel without having your feelings projected on to them.

It's like the time Kevin had driven into town to see the kids. Keep in mind he hadn't seen them in a month. Saturday morning, he got up and took them hiking. He packed sandwich stuff, but didn't let them eat it and made them wait until dinner. While he was in the grocery store, the kids said his girlfriend snuck them bread. The fun activity he planned for them that afternoon after hiking all day included pulling over on the side of the road, handing them each a trash bag, and making them all pick up trash. At times like that, I have to agree with my children. It's weird, and he's a jerk.

When they told me they were starving and on the side of the road picking up trash, I was tempted to drive by and throw cheeseburgers out the window at them. I chose to stay out of it though, which was a very hard choice. It took A LOT of *self-restraint*. I wanted to scratch his eyes out. My natural instinct when someone messes with my children is to become the lioness protecting my cubs. I know it's my job to protect my children, but I also don't have any control over what he does with them when he has them. That's a right you *lose* when you get divorced.

Truth is, whenever I did try, it only ended up making it worse on the kids, as Kevin took it out on them. They weren't going to actually starve, even though they may have felt like it for a short period of time. They were fed *eventually*, and it didn't hurt them to pick up trash. It was gross, and I would've preferred for them to wear gloves.

How you can make a 2-year-old pick up filthy trash that doesn't belong to you? I will probably never understand. I can tell you it did not leave any sort of impact on him, as I have seen him open a wrapper time and time again and drop it on the floor while talking to me. Seriously. The real question is, why you would want to spend the one weekend you see your kids that month torturing them? I haven't a clue. They *survived* it though. What's the saying…what doesn't kill you makes you stronger?

Maybe I should've protected them more. Deep down, I know I should have. I was scared of Kevin, I didn't want to deal with him, and I wanted him to go away. The more reaction he got from me, the worse he acted. The *crazier* he became. It was fear. So I chose to stay out of it; I would not let him see the torment he was causing me. After all, that's what he wanted. I was a chicken. I should've stood up for my babies, no matter what it cost me. I don't know that it would've made a difference, but at least I wouldn't have regret. I don't know that I could've actually done anything about it legally. They survived it, and they've learned how to stand up for themselves. Staying out of it, however, did actually help things somewhat improve over the long haul.

I think you have to come to the realization you have no control of what your ex is doing with your children, unless he/she is harming them. You could always call CPS or the police as long as you have a valid complaint you can prove. By all means, you sure as hell better intervene if your child is being *physically* harmed. I didn't see how I could prove the mental anguish he caused my children. He would always have an excuse and nothing would ever be his fault. Kevin sure as hell would've denied he ever said or did anything wrong.

I bring this up not because my ex has ever physically harmed my children, but because I worked with a lady in the Houston area that let her boyfriend brutally rape and murder her 4-

year-old daughter. I can't begin to imagine how someone could let something like that happen to their own child, and how her ex-husband must feel, not even knowing she was dating anyone…or knowing but not doing anything about it. It's *horrid,* and most of us could never understand how anyone could hurt a child. It happens though. None of us think it will be us, or our loved ones.

I think there is a fine line. You can't control if they feed them, what activities they choose to do with them, or what activities they make them miss. You have to talk to your kids though. You need to know what's going on when they are with your ex and whom they are around. They need to know it's not okay for someone to touch them inappropriately or hurt them, and if they do, they need to tell you. They can't be scared and we can't be scared to do anything about it. We can't cower down in order to avoid problems or drama. We just have to know the *difference* between someone placing our child in actual harm and us just not agreeing with the way we parent. You have to pick and choose your battles without putting the kids in the middle of it.

I got my kids a cell phone, even though my oldest was only 9, so they could call me anytime. We hid the phone in their bag, along with snacks so they could eat when they were hungry. You are their protector. It is your job to keep them safe. It is a very fine line with divorce, especially if you aren't the crazy one. So much control is lost. It's hard not to be able to shelter the people you love most from the evil in this world. Unfortunately, however, we can't. We lose all control over what happens when we get divorced. They don't have to feed them 3 meals a day, put them to bed at a certain time, or restrict their TV shows, movies, and social media. There is no law that says we have to parent the same, do holidays the same, and discipline the same; that part is up to us.

We have to be adults. The lucky ones can reach agreements. Work together. Others are going to make sure they do the opposite because they're assholes, and they can. All we can do is pray for our children. Pray for their safety, pray for the people caring for them, pray God wraps them in His armor and allows them to feel His love while they're away. Know that He is with us; He will never leave us nor forsake us, and He will protect us and our children.

# EMPTY NESTERS

## *MY FAVORITE ANTIDEPRESSANT*

Learning to be alone SUCKS. We were stuck living in Houston waiting for the divorce to finalize. We knew we had to make the best of it. We had to find a way to move forward. I could not just lie down and LET the little prick win. My sister and I had a rule: If we didn't have the kids, we were going out! The party was getting started.

I had a very difficult time with my kids being gone. In fact, I was clueless about how to live without them. They had been my entire life for the past 10 years. I had no hobbies, no interests, other than my kids. Our life consisted of ball games, practices, playing at the park, playing Barbie's, dress up, driving cars, coloring, and the list could go on and on. Common theme— nothing on the list is an adult activity. What are you supposed to do when you are being *forced* to take a break from something you don't want a break from? It took everything I had to not throw myself down every time they left and cry for hours. I literally wanted to act like a two-year-old and kick and scream. Throwing objects wildly around the house would've worked also; it is so hard to be the adult sometimes.

Rather than acting like the child I SO preferred, I *sulked* my sorrows in retail therapy and a night out on the town with my sister and girlfriends. As much as I would've rather had the kids for the weekend, I have to admit, it was a *blast*! I used to go out some in college but I never really had the opportunity to experience the single nightlife. After all, I did get married when I was 18. I had missed the typical college life. I had never known what it was like to go out on the town when you're single, and an adult. The possibilities were endless.

It was great getting all dressed up, heading downtown to the latest hip clubs, bars, and parties! Do people still use the word hip? I got hit on left and right, too! It was *crazy*, and girl did it make me feel good about myself; especially after the mental beat down I had been going through the past several years. A guaranteed injection of self-esteem! I was not about to let him get the best of me. As much as it hurt, and as much as I wanted to sit at home and sulk, I WOULD have a good time. I would make the best of it. It's crazy how you get so busy being a wife and a mother that you *forget* you're a person too. You have needs, desires, and wants. There's nothing wrong with that. You're not just someone's wife or mother; you are a person! You forget what it feels like to get noticed and to get male attention. The feeling of being revitalized, young, and wanted is amazing.

Another firm belief I have, drink plenty of wine!! There is *nothing* a couple of glasses can't cure, at least for a little while anyways. It's the world's greatest antidepressant. A glass or two in the evening, and everything looks a little brighter. Nothing seems quite so hopeless. I'd never really liked wine or beer, and mainly stuck with vodka and sprite or some kind of fruity mixed drink. Yes, I was one of those girls. It had to be sweet, fruity, and go down easy. After Kevin moved out, my little sister insisted I just hadn't tried the right kind. So we began tasting different kinds until I found several that I thoroughly enjoyed. Top suggestions: Moscato and Riesling (these are both sissy wines, a *great* starting place). The deal with wine is, after the first glass, *every* glass after goes down like water. Plus, it is meant to be sipped; not gulped, a hard change for me to make.

After the kids would go to bed or nights when they were with my ex, we would sit outside in the Jacuzzi and guzzle back the wine. After a couple glasses, I didn't have a care in the world, and I knew *everything* was going to work out. We would be okay. We would laugh for hours and hours. It felt great, and was a much needed release. After all, they say laughter is the best medicine! Relaxing and learning to let go can be difficult. With all the stress between bills, the divorce, and dealing with Kevin, unwinding and not thinking about it was exactly what I needed.

It may seem strange of me to be advising alcohol, considering that it was a large part of the problem with my marriage. Several key differences here; I didn't use it to function, I did not consume it on a regular basis, there was no mixing with prescription medications, no driving after drinking, no drinking while caring for my children, I could still walk and talk…I could go on and on and on. It's called self-control. I used it to relax, unwind, let go of the daily stress, and to most importantly *I used it to laugh.*

Exercise, exercise, exercise. I turned into a miniature version of Forest Gump. I went running all the time along some local jogging paths close to the house. Nothing like exercise to help the good endorphins kick in; come on stress relief! I ran almost every day, or at least went to the gym and worked out when I needed the daycare. Don't get me wrong, I am not an exercise addict. I love exercise, just not as much as I love wine, food, my friends, or just sitting on the couch on my ass, but *everyone* needs an outlet.

When you have kids, you can't sit around and cry, or drink for that matter, all the time. Although I am a total foodie, and the last thing I needed to do was sit around and eat. You have to be strong and courageous and set a good example for your kids. You have to find a way to be mentally healthy. Unfortunately, we can't stay drunk and party all the time, or we can't be the type of parents our children need. A *positive* outlet is a must!

Don't get me wrong, there were plenty of times I cried. I just didn't let myself sink into a deep, dark place that would be hard to crawl out of, and exercise was a Godsend for that. You have to find ways to keep going. You can't let that asshole affect you any longer, and it's hard not to, especially when your kids are gone. I mean it's truly SO unfair. They're selfish, they fuck it all up, and you have to hand your kids over kicking and screaming. Someone has to be the adult, and it's you, you get to be the rock for the kids. Kids need stability; be their person, the one they can *always* count on. You have to take time to find yourself, feel good about yourself, and be healthy. Exercise is important whether its running, swimming, biking, aerobics it doesn't matter. It's a great outlet, it's healthy and it will make you *feel* good, even if you aren't motivated. Push yourself. Take a walk with a girlfriend or ride bikes with your kid. The end results are truly a blessing.

Dealing with my kids being gone was one of the hardest things I've ever faced, but I thank God every day I have three beautiful, healthy, happy children. I would take having to share my children with my incredibly awful, arrogant ex over having a child that is sick or worse, any day. It's all about perspective. You just have to try and approach it with a positive attitude and surround yourself with supportive friends and family. A good support system is key! We all have hardships we have to deal with in life. We can't forget, however, that God will *never* give us more than we can handle. Although there may be times it seems questionable, He will not leave us nor forsake us. He will see us through to the other side. He will place people and opportunities in our lives when we need them. We have to trust Him and know that He will provide.

## TRUST AND OBEY

Faith. I don't see how someone could get through this process without faith. I know God loves me and wants me to be happy. During this process, I gained a relationship with the Lord I had never experienced before. God does not cause divorce. He doesn't cause people to hurt us. He cries for us through our pain, just as we would for our children. He loves and will provide for us. We have to turn it over to Him. We have to listen for His direction, in His time. Trust and obey, for there's no other way.

After I caught Kevin with the hooker, I felt like God wanted me to stay, and I did. I tried to listen. I spent countless hours in prayer for help, clarity, peace, and the ability to see the truth. *"Lord, if he is never going to change and things are never going to be different, please send me a sign."* I prayed for our relationship, for forgiveness, and for Kevin to be able to face his demons. After the drinking continued, I finally knew in my heart it was time to leave. I felt as though God was saying, you've done your part. You've tried. Now go and make a new life for yourself and your children. Cheesy? Maybe. I knew, however, that God was with me throughout the entire process, and no matter how tough it was, He was going to pull me through. I would be okay. He will never leave me nor forsake me, and He never has.

I'm not trying to say God encourages divorce by any means. Sometimes, however, there are circumstances that are unhealthy we do not need to be in. Circumstances in which that other person has been taken a hold of by Satan, and God does not cause that. People make their own choices. It's called Free Will. It creates circumstances that stand in the way of our own relationship with God. He will always forgive us and carry us through to the other side of whatever challenges we face, as long as we put our trust in Him. That's why I am where I am today. I give all the credit to God. He gave me strength, encouragement, and placed people in my path that I needed to be where I am today. For that, I am so thankful.

I'm not perfect. I'm a sinner just like Kevin. I make mistakes. I gossip, I curse too much and I get angry and resentful. The list would be a mile long if I sat down and was truly honest with myself. God loves us though our mistakes and imperfections. He will guide us through all our trials and tribulations as long as we turn it all over to Him. We have to listen. We have to be available and take the time to listen, to be engaged, and to hear His plan. You can't go wrong if you're following the path God chose for you. It doesn't matter what other people think or say. They aren't walking in your shoes, they don't know what you've been through, and they aren't the one that has to live with it. You are the only one that has to understand it and be willing to change your plan in order to fulfill his.

# FIRST OF MANYS

Going through a divorce leaves you to face many firsts you hadn't planned – first anniversary you don't spend together, first Christmas alone, first birthday as a single woman… I think you get the picture. It's an odd experience. You don't want to be with that person, much less miss them, but here's this date. This date used to be a big deal. It used to matter. Now it's just a date of would have beens. This would have been 15 years. The first year is probably the oddest. Emotions may range from sadness, to anger, to indifference. A bitter reminder of what life was supposed to be. As time goes on, however, it happens. It does become just another day.

*The first Christmas alone was heart wrenching.* For me, it was the absolute worst. Christmas morning for my family is HUGE. It's basically the only holiday we really care about celebrating. Christmas without kids just plain SUCKS. Strong suggestion; make alternate plans. DO

NOT spend it alone. Don't do your usual family gathering if you're without children. It doesn't get any more depressing than that. This is rock bottom, post-divorce. This is the one-day you will question yourself and your choices. You will not see your kids' faces Christmas morning. You will miss their eyes lighting up and the excitement on their faces. He will probably ruin it. It will not be the same experience for them either. They will probably sit in a circle and pass around a baby doll that they are supposed to pretend is baby Jesus. They will think it's weird. He will try to start new traditions and will not honor any traditions you may have shared as a family. It will be painful. Call a friend and pretend that it isn't Christmas. You will thank me; trust me, don't torture yourself.

*It was my first birthday after my divorce.* I was 28, divorced with 3 kids, and living with my parents. Loser Alert. OMG it was depressing! It felt like I had gone backwards. I had accomplished nothing. I had nothing to show for my life thus far. I was alone; I didn't have my own house, savings, or a plan for that matter. I was in survival mode. My parents always said one kid would move back home, one kid would get pregnant before they get married, and one kid would get divorced. Those are the statistics of our society. I was the statistic for our family— you're welcome sisters! I took care of everything for all three of us. For that, y'all are welcome. Enjoy your long marriages. Thanks to me, you did not get pregnant before you got married and you never have to move in with mom and dad. I like to think I took one for the team.

*First birthday of your child's that you miss.* Standard divorce decree gives the non-custodial parent visitation on their child's birthday. Therefore, you no longer get to spend their birthday with them. Yes, another hard one to swallow. Once again, the jackass wins. Your kids don't get a party on their actual birthday and they will spend the day with an egotistical, selfish asshole that doesn't care about anyone but themselves. You will spend the day thinking about the fact you carried them for 9 months, survived delivering them, and have cared for them every day of their lives since and you don't get to spend the anniversary of that day with them, even though you were the one that *actually* did all the work on that day. They over took your body and you blew up like an elephant. Your body was never the same. It is now covered in tiger stripes, loose skin, and things didn't quite go back where they started. You developed hemorrhoids, can't jump without peeing yourself, and now have breasts that point south like deflated balloons – and while your body is now a representation of your love for them, they spend the day with the asshole whose body didn't go through shit. Not fair. This day *sucks* too.

*First time you meet the new girlfriend is also a good one.* On this day, you'll want to knock the smug look off the jerk's face. She will likely be genuine. She thinks they have something special and she is here to save the day. She is eager, likely very young, and unaware of the situation she has gotten herself into. She will learn. She will one day be standing in your shoes. So be nice and take pleasure in knowing she will be you in 10 years…. if she lasts that long. If she's smart, she will figure him out and dump him anyways. There's really no point in being ugly. Most importantly, remember no one can replace you to your children. You are their mother. She cannot, and will not replace you. It does not matter how young or cute she is; your children love you more. So shake it off, pull up your *big girl panties*, and show them both you don't give a shit. You are not intimidated. They DO NOT matter.

*First time to attend a school event as the "single mom."* Don't be alarmed. Yes, it feels like everyone is staring at you and yes, they probably are. Some are probably judging you, others are feeling sorry for you, and the majority may appear to be staring at you when in all actuality they really do not care. Most people don't care unless it affects them directly. No matter what you've done or had done to you, most people do not care. So hold your head up high. Enjoy your precious child and whatever you may be watching them do. They are all that matters. Yes, you may be by yourself, but be proud. You are independent, happy, and no longer living a lie. Half of these other women are still in it. They are shallow and lonely, judging you helps them to feel a little better about themselves. Just let them have it.

*First time going to church as a single mom.* Here you are sitting with your three unruly children, or worse, you are ALONE. Here sit all these happily married families—husbands, wives, and children. Throughout the ceremony, you see the "parental" looks. One child winds up seated between the parents after he is reprimanded for talking, pushing, or shoving his brother. Once you no longer have that, you realize how big those small moments were. You no longer have a parental partner. You are alone, trying to parent the best you can. Trying to make it through church and focus on what is most important, your *relationship* with God. All you really are focused on is what you don't have. While all you may see around you are the other families, which is not the case at all. These people are our brothers and sisters in Christ. They are hurting and wounded just like you. They may have just lost a loved one or received a terminal diagnosis. They may be having marital problems just like you. Do not be *discouraged* my friend, this too shall pass.

*First time going out as a single woman.* This is HUGE. The newfound freedom bestowed upon you is terrifying. If you get hit on, you are free to react in any fashion you deem fit. You can talk to any man you want. The safety net of, *"I'm sorry, I don't think my husband would appreciate that,"* is gone. While this can be a good thing, you are in new territory. The last thing you want is to jump into a new relationship, but the flattery of new male attention…. let's just say there's nothing like it. I remember this night like it was yesterday. My sister insisted that if we were going out on the town, I had to wear heels. Let me just say, I have never been a *heels* kind of girl. Tennis shoes, flip-flops, a dressy sandal, maybe a cute flat at most. That's all I'd ever worn. No, they don't lengthen the leg and draw the sex appeal that the right heel can, but I couldn't walk in a heel without looking like a penguin. They kill my feet. It does not matter how expensive, how tall, how short, after a couple hours, I'm done. By the end of the night, I walked barefoot through the streets of Houston. I didn't care. All I wanted to do was get those stupid shoes off and get home to my bed. I had fun, don't get me wrong, and I learned that for men with a foot fetish, my game was spot on. TBH I know I have pretty feet; however, I think it's creepy you noticed and now I'm not interested. If I could do that night again, I would've worn a wedge and something I felt comfortable in. You gotta be comfortable to get your game on, right?

*First time on a blind date.* Blind dates can be the *worst.* I don't think it really matters if it's someone you met online or through a friend. It is nerve wracking. The worst part is probably when there is no attraction to that person at all. You are trying, trying to get to know them and trying to give them the benefit of the doubt. Seriously, you're not a miracle worker. There's either a spark or there isn't. Worst case, it's an awkward night out away from the kids with another adult. Yes, conversation can be a struggle, but most people like to talk about themselves. Asking questions will usually get you through the night. If not, there's always Plan B— the infamous phone call "the kids are sick" and you have to go home. Everyone should be able to take a hint at that point. You're not interested; there will be no second date. My first blind date was a group setting. It wasn't so much a blind date as an opportunity to check each other out. The guy was totally not my type. I can be shallow; I'll admit it. I found his looks repulsive, and I never gave him a chance. I couldn't. I am just not into the long hair cowboy with the half unbuttoned shirt. Thanks but no thanks. Luckily, it was a group setting, so the night was still fun. I'm sure I seemed like a total bitch, but honestly, it was true.

*First time living by yourself.* Sometimes female equality isn't what it's cut out to be. Don't get me wrong, I'm glad we can vote, work, and have the same rights. I would love to be able to say a woman can do anything a man can, but there are some jobs that *only* a man should do. I don't want to plunge a stopped up toilet, unclog a stopped up drain, bury a dead animal, or basically take care of any household repair, leak, or problem. I want a man to do it for me. I guess I am just one of those women. Give me an apron and cast iron skillet and I will gladly play the part to avoid doing some nasty, or worse, complicated home repair. I had just gotten the kids a new kitten. It was tiny and adorable. I mean, really, is there anything cuter than a kitten? I think not. We were backing out of the driveway to go get pizza, and it happened. I ran over the kitten. I know what you're thinking; believe me. I've thought it myself. I tried to call my dad, but he was out of town and wouldn't be back until that evening. I could not face it. I didn't want to see that sweet baby kitten I had just flattened like a pancake, much less touch it, or bury it. So, not wanting to draw to much attention to it, I went on in to town to pick up the pizza. When I got there, the owner came to the window. He and I have been friends since we were kids. So naturally when he asked how I'd been? I BROKE DOWN. I had just *killed* my kid's kitten. She was still lying in the driveway. I didn't want to go home. I was freaking out. Thank the Lord he's a nice guy. He followed me home, and while I took the kids and pizza inside, he buried the kitten in the backyard. And that ladies, is one reason why it is nice to have a man around. As soon as I figure out reason #2...... I'll let you know.

*First time having the flu.* Being sick with no back up or help is the worst. Here you are, feeling like you're dying, but you can't because you have these tiny humans you are responsible for. Here is this child that cannot care for himself. He is in diapers and basically helpless, even though he's almost 3. He is a male and we all know that will never get better. My daughters, at the time, would've been 7 and 10. Yes, they are willing to help as long as they have nothing better to do. You are weak, you feel like you're dying, and your strength to argue with them has left your body. So here you are sweating with chills, all the while cooking, bathing, dressing, and caring for these children, who will never appreciate it, in between trips to the toilet so you can vomit or have diarrhea. It is terrible and some of the worst days you will encounter. Luckily, it will be a blur. You won't remember much of it. Dig deep ladies. You will survive it.

*First vacation.* We had always gone on a family vacation, every summer, that's what the kids and I were used to. Things at the time were different; the divorce had taken quite a strain on the entire family. It's not that we didn't get along; frankly, I think we all just needed a break. I needed a change from the usual group venture. I did NOT however, want to go it alone. It made me nervous to go visit an unfamiliar place alone with three kids, but I didn't want to let them down. I was not about to let being single prevent me from taking my kids on vacation! Being single, I couldn't afford much either. So I did the next best thing, I got together with 2 of my girlfriends and their children. We loaded up and drove to Hot Springs, Arkansas. We rented a timeshare that would sleep us all, 3 adults and 10 children. We spent the week hanging out, taking the kids to the lake, and going to see all the sites Hot Springs has to offer. It was *miserably* hot in July, but we had a blast. That's what mattered. To this day, the kids remember it being one of their favorite vacations. It just goes to show you it's not about what you spend or where you go, it's whom you're with and the memories you make.

# SINGLE AND READY TO MINGLE

Now the chapter you've all been waiting for…
the exciting life of the "single mom." Say what?
Wild nights, parties, secret rendezvous,
glamorous trips. It is finally my time!  Don't I
wish, if only it were that glamorous.  No, this is
the chapter in which I tell you about all my stupid
choices and decisions.  Some I wish I could take
back, some I'm glad I experienced, and some I
would do better at if I had a do-over.  I'm sharing
this because you are going to make stupid choices
too.  None of us are perfect, and when you do,
and you're feeling like a piece of dirt on the
ground beneath everyone else, this will be your
chapter.  This will make you feel like you're not
alone.  You aren't the only one with the not so
bright ideas.  You have these thoughts, feelings,
and desires that no longer have to be stuffed
away— filed in a place we never visit.  Nope.
Neverland is here.  This is your time to
experience what you may or may not have when

you were younger. Those "what if" moments your mind would drift to, while you were stuck in your loveless marriage. This is your chance to get it right. You HAVE to experience a few Mr. Wrongs before you ever find Mr. Right.

When Kevin and I first separated, the last thing I wanted to think about was dating. I had just ended a 10-year marriage. I had been married since I was 18 years old for Pete's sake. I just wanted to be. I wanted to be a good person, a good mom, and a chance to be me. Although it was not on my priority list at the time, there was always that *little voice* in the back of my mind wondering if I would ever meet anybody. Was Kevin right? Would anyone ever want someone with three kids? Would anyone want me? Would I have to settle for some old, fat, bald guy? Would I be like my ex mother-in-law and forever be an old spinster? Everyone tells you that you will meet the right person and deserve better, but was it REALLY true? I honestly wasn't too sure about it at all.

Things with Kevin had been bad for so long it was such a relief when it was finally over. There were no tears, no regrets, and no doubts. I had been grieving the loss of our marriage since I caught him with the hooker. By the time we separated, all I felt was relief. I think most of us grieve the ending of a marriage like the loss of a loved one. The battle has been lost, and the marriage is dead. I lived in denial for two years after I caught him with a hooker. I wanted to *believe* he would change. If I am honest with myself, I was living in denial long before I ever caught him. The anger came and went. There were times I remember just staring at him thinking how much I hated him. How it would take 20 years of him being perfect (at this point we all know what a joke that is) just to be able to not hate him. That day would never come.

I would bargain with God. Praying for him to tell me when it was time (as if there weren't enough reasons to leave already). I was constantly praying He would provide me with more signs that Kevin would never change. God basically had to hit me over the head for me to finally see it. I battled depression off and on the next few years, and I finally reached acceptance. I knew leaving was my only option and there would be no regrets. Getting rid of that lying, cheating bastard was the *best* decision I ever made. He was slicker than a greased pig at the county fair, always had been, always would be. It felt like a weight had been lifted off my shoulders…so much relief, I could finally breathe again. You live, you learn, and then you upgrade, which is exactly what I planned on doing.

*Lesson 1:* Learn how to date. I had no idea what I was doing or where to begin. After all, I had basically been with Kevin since I was 16. I wouldn't call that dating. Dating should really be like buying a car; you should get to talk to the previous owners. Show me the man fax! Ladies, we would really do ourselves a favor and save ourselves A LOT of heartache. Sure, you will always have the disgruntled ex, but it might help the next girl figure it out a little sooner. Why do women always assume the ex is just jealous? Why would she be jealous you are getting her sloppy seconds? She obviously didn't want him. Maybe we should open our eyes and listen; she may be trying to do us a favor. The thought of dating was frightening. I DID NOT want another Kevin. *A lot* had changed since I was a teenager. We now had cell phones, social media, and texting. I was an adult now. I was insecure and I didn't want to screw up. The good news was my ex had set the bar so low, anyone that hadn't slept with a hooker should basically be impressive.

*Lesson 2:* The thought of having sex with someone else, oh God help me! This was the most terrifying part. I didn't want anyone to see me naked. Don't get me wrong, I looked fine with clothes on, but I'd breastfed three kids. My boobs looked like two deflated balloons. If the lights were on, whomever I was with would see them. On the other hand, if the lights were off, they'd never find them. And the stretch marks,

OMG the stretch marks!! I had earned those tiger stripes, but really, who wants to see that? I could barely stand to look at them. My kids would yell "oooh gross" every time I changed in front of them! I couldn't imagine finding a man who would be able to look past them – a man who wouldn't look at my stomach and have to look away. After all, my stomach looked like an 18-wheeler had rolled over it and then peeled out…. several times! I wasn't quite sure how I was going to deal with all of this. I didn't really have a plan. Plastic surgery? Hmmm…boob job, tummy tuck? In my dreams, I couldn't afford it. I was just going to have to make do with what I had. If they couldn't deal with the battle scars I had endured, then they weren't worth wasting my time on (that's what I told myself anyway…repeatedly).

## GETTING YOUR FEET WET

*Step 1:* Get you a friend with benefits. The last thing you need is to jump into another long- term relationship. You need time to heal. Have some fun.  Just find a friend you can talk to and have fun with.  Someone you can work out those dating anxieties with and not worry about it getting serious.

I was still living in Houston, my divorce wasn't final, and I was basically stuck in this 60-day waiting period.  We had filed but had to wait the 60-day period and come to some sort of agreement before it would be finalized (it took 6 months, which was fast, all things considered).  There was a CRNA student at the hospital I worked at.  He was *always* flirting with me, and he was HOT. Like, out of my league hot.  He was a bit of a playboy, and I was good with that, the last thing I wanted was a relationship.  I would take the attention.  It was nice, if I do say so myself.

He eventually got my phone number and started texting me.  Dirty messages at that; there's a first time for everything I guess.  It was odd at first, I mean the last time I dated we didn't even have cell phones.  We had to use a landline, and there was no email. Other than a letter, you couldn't just write what you wanted. You had to actually say it out loud. I would play along; it felt so good to know another man would be interested in me. Maybe Kevin wasn't right after all? It continued on for a month or two, we went out a couple times, and it eventually fizzled out. It was the perfect example of a "*friend with benefits.*" No commitment. No feelings, just a little harmless flirting, with some benefits on the side, without having to worry about where it was leading. I definitely wasn't looking for anything serious. The last thing I wanted was to jump into another bad relationship. Obviously my picker was broken the first time, so I knew it needed a little time and TLC before it would work correctly. I needed some time to find myself and figure out what it was I wanted. Oddly enough, it wasn't something I had even considered for a very long time, if ever.

*Step 2:* Go have fun with your girlfriends. Quit taking life so serious. This is your time to cut loose.  Don't worry about finding *Mr. Right*. That will happen, all in good time.  Have fun and get out of the house.  It is time to get out of the sweatpants, ladies!  Put on something that makes you feel good.  Be confident.  Go have some fun and realize what all you have to offer.

For the next several months, my sister, our friends, and I would go out for a night on the town, whenever I didn't have the kids, of course. The nightlife of downtown Houston provided the entertainment we desperately needed, permitting us to attend various parties, clubs, bars, and openings.  I wouldn't say we always made the smartest decisions.  Like the time we nick named this guy "*Bubbles*" at a party we attended and let him drive our car around to all these different bars.  We had also made up fake names for ourselves.  I was *Lola* and my sister was *Gigi*. We were hilarious, if I do say so myself. That's how it usually happens—get a little alcohol in us and suddenly we are the life of the party, at least that's what we think, anyways.  But seriously, my sister is *hilarious*. She does this thing at bars where she goes up behind a random guy, squats down, and opens her mouth. When you snap a photo, it literally looks like she is eating his ass. It's something we like to call "*taking a bite out of crime*." The key is not to get caught, which would be oh so embarrassing. Although, I have to say, it has happened a couple of times. In that case, you have two plays— you're the drunk girl that didn't know what was happening or abort ship and get the heck out of there. It was quite the night with "Bubbles," luckily he didn't turn out to be an axe murderer either.

I finally learned the true meaning of beer goggles, although I'm not sure that's something to brag about. My sister and I were at a local pub by the house. We were engaged in a serious game of Ping-Pong that included no rules and basically allowed you to return the ball from any area in the bar. Looking back, I can't imagine how *annoying* we must've been. We didn't care though. We were there to have a good time, and frankly didn't care what anybody thought. There were a couple guys that had asked us to play pool, and we politely declined.  As the night continued on, and the drinks continued coming, we started to feel a little more daring and up to the challenge. Everyone in the bar started to look a little better, less trashy, and more attractive (you get the picture).  They asked us again, and we decided to join them.  After all, I had just defeated a girl in an arm wrestling match, which entitled me to another free drink, needless to say we were feeling pretty good.  I remember thinking to myself, *"They're really not as gross as I thought they were." "His middle section doesn't look quite so thick and the other guy's nose isn't quite as big as the state of Oregon."* The night continued on, and the drinks kept pouring in.  Finally, my sister excused herself to the bathroom.  On her way, an older gentleman intercepted her and said *"you girls are too cute for these guys.  It's time for y'all to go home."* Luckily my sister came to her senses, grabbed me, and made us leave, much to the guys' dismay. And that, my friend, is a perfect definition of *beer goggles*. I am so thankful we left.

*Step 3:* Have you gone out and had a little fun? Now it's time to think about dating. The hardest part about this is meeting someone. Be open to a blind date. Check out an online dating site. Remember, just because you date someone doesn't mean you have to marry them, much less ever talk to them again. Just relax and take it slowly. When you meet the right one, you'll know.

The divorce was finally final, and we moved back home, which meant all the going out and partying had come to an end. What happens in H town, stays in H town. Partly because Glendale was a small town, meaning your options were limited unless you wanted the entire town to know about every embellished detail of your evening. We were all starting over and getting our lives together. It was time to figure out what's what. Namely, who I was and what I wanted. There were a few blind dates here and there. I don't quite understand why people think just because they know someone that's single they should set you up, even though you're not remotely attracted to them and have absolutely nothing in common with them. Just being single is not a big enough common denominator!!

After one bad blind date after another, I decided I was finished with them. It was a waste of my time, evening, and a sitter. I wanted to know if I was attracted to someone or if I had anything in common with him before I wasted my time going out with him! So, I let my sisters talk me into trying the internet. Internet dating??? It seemed weird; after all, it's how my ex found a lot of the women he was with. That in itself made me feel *dirty* and *desperate*. Was it really for me? Although *leery*, I decided to give it a go, frightening as it was. After all, there were several couples I had heard of that it did work for, a couple of them I even knew. At that point, what did I have to lose? I was living in Glendale, a town with a whopping population of 3,000 people. I worked full time and took care of my three absolutely perfect children, how the hell else was I going to meet someone?

*Step 4:* Set some standards. What do you want out of a relationship? What do you NOT want? Make a list. There's nothing wrong with writing down what you want in a partner and what you absolutely will not tolerate. It's nice when you are questioning a relationship to go back and be able to put yourself in check.

Here's mine:

1. Christian – this was a must for me. Now don't get me wrong, Christianity is something we grow in constantly. He didn't have to be perfect, or be a priest for that matter. He had to be open to the possibility and willing to learn and grow in faith alongside me

2. Make a decent living (Nothing less than $75,000/year) – I'm not trying to sound like

a bitch. I am not interested in being the breadwinner. Life with three kids is a struggle. I am struggling with a college degree in a profession that does make that amount. The last thing I need is one more person to take care of. I didn't want to worry about money.

3. Family Man – Family first. I wanted someone who would always put family first. Someone who would put the needs of me and the kids above their own. I had done selfish, I didn't care to go backwards.

4. Has to have a good family – They don't have to have a perfect family. They just have to be nice, easy to deal with, and enjoyable to be around. I had already dealt with the in-laws that were selfish, only cared about themselves, and manipulative. Apples tend to not fall from the tree.

5. History of drug and alcohol abuse – No thanks

6. History of cheating – No thanks

7. Arrest record – No thanks

## *SHE PROMISED HERSELF BETTER*

I chatted with some guys here and there. It was nice to get some male attention, but most of all; I got to know them before wasting my time. If they seemed weird, or not quite my style, I could ex them off quickly. There were a couple that seemed somewhat interesting, and I finally decided to meet up with one. He was smoking HOT, and I was shocked when he actually sent me a message. We talked for several weeks *before* deciding to meet. I was so nervous. It was the first real date I had actually been on since I was in high school. I must have changed my outfit 100 times; you know how we do, ladies.

I was so anxious I had a glass of wine before I went. It was the only way I was going to be able to get out of my car and walk inside the restaurant where we were meeting. We met for dinner and drinks, and the date went great! It wasn't nearly as awkward as I thought it would be. I actually felt super comfortable with him, and he was *every* bit as good looking in person as he was in his picture…HUGE relief! After our date, however, he dropped a bombshell on me. Apparently he had received a DUI several months before and had to spend his weekends in jail. Seriously, I'm not even kidding. I FINALLY find a guy I sort of like and yep, jail on the weekends. Totally my luck. What the hell? Why do things *always* turn out this way?

Being the gullible, naïve person I am, or perhaps I should say desperate, I chose to see the good in him. Realistically, how many of us have gotten behind the wheel of a car after having a drink too many? I know I had. I had a glass of wine before I met him, had a couple drinks throughout the evening, and drove home! Is it fair to judge him just because he got caught? It seemed like it had been a wakeup call for him too, at least that's what he told me. I'm a Christian, I chose forgiveness, as it also benefited me. I ignored my list and we continued to date for about 5 months. There were some questionable incidents that occurred during that time, but for the most part, I was just having fun. I had no intention of ever introducing him to my children.

Even as much fun as we were having, I knew he wasn't anyone I *planned* on getting serious with. The red flags were becoming hard to ignore. He was just SO darn good looking and a blast to go out with, and really, that was all I needed during that time. The red flag finally became apparent, however, and it all came to an end.

We went and spent the weekend at his friend's house for the 4th of July. We had been there all day, and in the late evening he received a phone call from an "old friend". When he hung up the phone, he said he was worried about his friend and needed to go see him. He encouraged me not to come, and left. I'm not even shitting you. He left me all alone, with people I didn't even know, and had taken my car on top of that. I was finally able to fall asleep, only to wake up the next morning and realize he had never come back, nor had my car. I was stuck at some strange people's house with no idea where he was. I began *frantically* texting and calling; I was madder than a wet hen. What if he didn't come back? How did I let myself end up here again? He finally did; however, and that was the end of that relationship!!

After that, I decided I was going to be pickier, no more compromising my values. It was time to focus on other aspects of my life. I was going quit worrying about dating and being single. That would come when it was meant to happen. It was time to figure myself out. The focus needed to be on my job and most importantly my kids; I needed to get my shit straight. There would be no more men with a record, lesson learned. If the right guy came along, he came along. But for me, I would only be going out with friends if the kids were at their dads, no more sitters. I would only be going out to try and stay busy when my kids were gone. Having fun is important, but I needed to find me.  Not me with a boyfriend, but me as a person.  I needed to know what makes me tick, what I wanted from my life, and how I wanted to live my life.  What kind of *legacy* did I want to leave for my children?  I wasn't sure where to go from this point forward, but what I did know was I wanted to lead a life they could be proud of.

 I continued to go out with friends when the kids were at their dad's, and was still driving them to Houston the first weekend of every month. It was a great chance to see my old friends and work buddies.  Visiting a metropolitan area also allowed a little more privacy than a small town afforded.

One weekend while in Houston, I had gone to a party with some of my girlfriends.  It was at the house of a guy I previously worked with.  I was having such a blast with my old girlfriends; I had missed them terribly!  We ended up staying the night and I had my first and ONLY one-night stand with one of his friends!  The guy was really sweet and nice, but boy did I feel like a big, fat slut the next day! I had always wondered what it would be like to have a *one-night stand*. I missed out on the college years, and not that I felt like that was part of it, but it is part of it for a lot of people. The real problem was I was NOT 20 years old and though I was single, I was a mother of three children. I was not liking the person I was becoming. This was only further confirmation it was time to get straight. I knew it was time for me to get my life together, decide what was *important*, and focus my actions on getting on track.

I needed to find myself. For the past 10 years, I had been a wife, mother, student, nurse, etc. I had no idea who I was. I had no idea what I wanted. I didn't know how to be comfortable in my own skin. I didn't know how to respect myself. So I worked and worked, ran my kids around, went to church, and put the worry of men and being a single mother out of my head. I needed to stay busy. There is no place more dangerous than that of an idle mind. It was time to do me.

One night, I remember having a serious talk with God. I told him, *"I didn't want to be a single mother forever, but I want to live my life according to Your will."* I just prayed that when the time was right, He would place a godly man in my life. I gave my worries to Him. I knew God wanted me to be happy, and He would provide everything I needed in His timing. After all, He had seen me through thus far, even though all I had done was abandon Him in order to serve myself. I could do this, and I certainly didn't need a man to take care of me. It was time to trust in Him, my way wasn't getting me anywhere. After all, look where the last one left me.

## *HIM*

About six months later, I received a call from a guy one of my friends had set me up with previously. We had gone on a blind date with my girlfriend and her husband 4 or 5 months earlier and I had never heard from him again. Although weird, not a big deal, it was one blind date and we didn't even really speak to each other. I wasn't sure, however, if I even wanted to talk to him. After all, he had blown me off before. But he was SOOO cute. The first time we met he was separated, and his divorce was to become final in the weeks to follow. We all know the drama and complications that go along with divorce. Maybe there was more to it? I had *assumed* he just wasn't into me. But maybe that wasn't it after all.

He started calling me. We talked every day on the phone for hours upon end. I don't think I had spoken on the phone like that since junior high; I felt like a *school girl*. We would spend hours on the phone every evening—talking about life, telling silly stories from our pasts, and just about anything else we could come up with. We tried to get together once a week, mainly when I didn't have the kids, even if it was simply just driving around talking. In Texas, we like to do a little thing called *back-roading*, where we drive around on all the back, country roads. Lame as it may sound; if I was with him, it was more than appealing.

He was so different from anyone I'd ever been with. He wanted to know everything about me, down to the smallest detail. He loved to listen to me talk and tell stories. I don't think I'd ever had someone so interested in what I had to say. We had a lot in common and a lot of the same goals and values. In my heart, I knew he was the man God had sent, and he was *exactly* what I needed. He was so attentive, and it was such a nice change. Imagine, a man that actually put your wants and needs before his own? Crazy, right?

I remember on one of our first dates, he came over and I cooked dinner. After a few glasses of wine, I decided it would be a great idea to go show off on the trampoline I had just bought for my kids. Who even does that, seriously? This girl here does. Never mind the fact I was almost 30, apparently wine gives me *superpowers.*

Needless to say, I made a complete ass out of myself. I attempted a front flip. Much to my dismay, wanting to ensure that it was impressive, I *overdid* it. The flip turned into a one and a half, which resulted in my face slamming into the metal railing and plastic slide (the kids had pushed up next to the trampoline so they could climb on easily). Can you say, humiliating? I was just lying there, completely humiliated and he was speechless. My head was pounding, and neither of us knew what to say. After a couple minutes, he finally said *"Are you okay?"* Then, we both laughed hysterically. When he stuck around after that, with my black eye and all, I knew we had something special! After several months of dating and huge conversations to follow, we decided to take things to the next step and introduce him to my kids.

# GETTING WHAT YOU WANT

*"Someday everything will all make perfect sense. So for now, laugh at the confusion, smile through the tears, and keep reminding yourself everything happens for a reason."*

I think introducing your kids to a man you are dating is a HUGE step! You certainly should not introduce them to every Tom, Dick, and Harry you date, but when is the *right* time? I spent A LOT of time praying about it all.

After the first couple of dates with Derek, I knew deep down he was IT. I felt like God had answered my prayers and sent me a good, Christian man. I wouldn't say I loved him at that moment, but I did know I wanted more with him. More time with him, more of a commitment, more... I was ready for more. We had been dating for about 3 months. We talked on the phone every night, but only saw each other on the weekends my kids were gone to their dads and occasionally when my mom would watch them. Things were rocking along rather nicely, and we decided (with strong encouragement from me, of course) it was time to take the next step.

## IT'S A BALANCING ACT

This was it; we were finally doing it. Derek was coming over to my house for dinner, and this would be his first night to meet the children. My daughter's friend that lived across the street was also over. She wanted to make sure she got to meet him too, and we always had extras over. I was inside cooking spaghetti when I saw him pull up. I was nervous. Would the kids be too much? Would they like him? Would he like them? After tonight, would I ever see him again? Was this too fast? All of the sudden, all four kids (my three + the neighbor) went running outside and bombarded him before he could even get in the door. Oh *wow,* not the first impression I was hoping for.

It began to stress me out a little, you know that feeling when you start turning red, sweat in places you shouldn't, and your heart is racing ninety to nothing. I was beginning to freak, but I thought to myself…. if he can't handle this, then this isn't going to work anyways. I repeated it, over and over and over, until I was convinced. The reality is, I have three kids and our life is pure chaos! I wouldn't have it any other way. They are my *everything*. Take it or leave it. Luckily, the night went rather well, and he and the kids got along great. After that night, I knew he was the one for sure. After you see a man with your children, it's hard to not fall for him. That's exactly why I always try and warn people, *"don't introduce your children until you are sure about the man you're dating because it is only going to make you fall harder for them."*

One night I had sent the kids to my parents for a sleep over. Derek and I had a date that evening, the plan was, I would pick them up before church. Little did I know my mother had to be at the 8:30 service, which meant they were left alone with my dad.  Don't get me wrong, my dad is a pretty awesome man.  He does not, however, do well with small children.  Then came the phone call, *"Hurry up and come get your kids."*  Well, of course, I didn't want them to realize I had been with Derek and he stayed over!  So, naturally, I took my time to tell him goodbye. Here it comes, my loving father called a second time, *"Come get you god damn kids now!"*  My car was at my parents' house, which meant I had to walk.  Derek had already pulled off.  So here I am, pajamas and all.  My father at this point had foam coming out of his mouth; he was so pissed off.  He was done watching them and had flipped his lid.  So, I gathered the kids up as quickly as possible and we headed down the driveway, following my father out.  He heads out the gate, which is electric, and I am so close behind him and half frazzled from the morning, I went ahead and followed.  BAM! Apparently, the gate was closing and the force of my car actually bent the gate in half.  It was the icing on the cake!  I couldn't believe my eyes. I was crying. My dad was now laughing. It was *insanity* at its finest, story of my life.

My knight in shining armor had finally arrived! If only it were that simple. It's a hard adjustment bringing someone new into your children's lives. It's an adjustment for everyone. It was an adjustment for Derek because he didn't have any children and had to get used to three, at various ages, all at the same time. He was taking on an instant family, or attempting to anyways. Did I mention Derek was also 3 years younger than me? He was maybe all of 16 when my oldest daughter was born. He did not have the *first clue* about parenting! As every parent knows, parenting is a process. It takes time to figure it out. Every child is different and has to be handled accordingly. Luckily, we have years to figure it out, and we might actually get it right by the last one. Bringing someone knew into your kids' lives is a huge adjustment for them too! After all, here is someone new, coming into their lives, taking on a parental role—only he's not their parent (or step parent) for that matter.

By this point, the kids were used to it being just us. Let's face it, moms are typically more of the push over. It's only fair to mention I may have over compensated for my divorce with my kids by always trying to fix things for them. If they were sad, I wanted to make it better. I wasn't always as strict or consistent as I should've been, which of course didn't make it any easier for Derek. It really didn't benefit my children either. I think it taught them a little bit about manipulating the situation to get what they want. I think it is vital for both people to handle discipline, but you have to be on the same page. You have to start slow and let them ease into it. On the one hand, it is hard to let someone else discipline your children, but how can you expect someone to be around your children all the time without any control over your children's behavior? It takes time to work out all of the kinks; in fact, I really think it's a never-ending process. You just have to find what works for everyone, if that's really even possible. Anyone with children and stepchildren knows exactly what I'm talking about. It's the main source of conflict, and it's a continuous process.

My son was almost 4 and mostly potty-trained, but he was TERRIBLE at wiping, as most small children are. Derek was home with the kids, and Cooper pooped. Derek was determined he was going to wipe himself and he would teach him. So here he is hunched over, and instructing him. Copper goes back to wipe, pulls his hand forward, swinging it toward Derek, and there it is, a big glob of poop on his finger. Out of reaction, Derek hits his hand knocking it back on to Coopers face. Welcome to parenting.

*Issue #1.* Derek and I continued dating for almost a year. There were *plenty* of ups and downs. There were some core differences that took some adjusting. For example, church for me was huge. I had grown up going to church every Sunday. I think church is great for a reset. It keeps you focused on what's important. I don't think you have to go to church to be a Christian, but going reminds you of what your focus for each week should be. It keeps me grounded and it gives you a community. I wanted my kids to have that. My mom engrained it in our heads. You go to church on Sundays, no matter what. It is hard to make your children go if your spouse doesn't. More importantly, it's hard to make a marriage work if it isn't centered on God. A family that prays together, stays together. Derek was a Christian, no doubt about it. He hadn't, however, grown up in a church. It was something I needed. I needed us to be a family that put faith first if this was going to work, and going to church was part of it. All it took was explaining my feelings to him and he was all for it. Sundays are my favorite days.

*Issue #2.* Attendance of the kids' activities. This was new for Derek. He didn't have kids and wasn't used to spending his evenings at practices and ball games. I'd been doing it for the past 10 years. It's important to be a presence in your kids' lives. I think we, as parents, should go support them in everything they do. Unless you are sick or working, I don't see what else is more important. Once again, I expressed my concerns, and Derek was receptive. He would be at everything unless he was working. They already had a father that attended nothing. The last thing they needed was a step dad that did the same.

Our first Christmas with Derek's family was one for the books. I would say we made quite an impression. We were going to his family Christmas at his grandmother's house on his dad's side. We had not met anyone on that side. Of course, I loved his parents and sister right from the start. Upon entering the house, we met his grandmother. She says, and I quote, *"Well, aren't you girls pretty, you must take after your grandmother!"* Well okay, this is going to be good. Derek had a cousin in his 30's and one that was about 10 at the time. They had been building this huge Lego dinosaur; it must've taken hours.

It was in the back bedroom where everyone was placing their coats. Yes, my daughter knocked it over and broke it when she went to put up her coat. Way to make a first impression. We survived dinner and presents. Things seemed to be going better. And then it happened, a fist-fight arose between my girls. Right there, in the middle of everyone. That was it. Three strikes, we were out of there. At least Derek's parents got a kick out of it. According to them it was the most exciting Christmas they'd had in a while!

We had talked about marriage and our plans for the future numerous times. We knew this was something we both wanted. It was October, and Derek and I were going out for the night. I was inside getting all dolled up, and he was outside in the garage messing with my lawn mower. For real, we were going out; he arrived late, so WHY would he be messing with the lawn mower? I was *so annoyed*. He kept calling my cell phone and telling me to come outside. Good Gosh man, I'm trying to get ready! Irritated, I walked into the garage and there he was, bent down, on the other side of the lawn mower, on one knee. It was a surprise to say the least, and not what I was expecting at all!

He told me he loved me, that he knew I was the woman for him, and asked me to marry him. Wow! I knew it was coming, but I was expecting something along the lines of a nice dinner! This was SO much better. The ring was gorgeous, as knew it would be (after all, I picked it out, something else I was getting right this time). He was late getting there because he had stopped by my parents' house to ask for their permission. That meant so much to me, and to them I know. It may not sound like the most romantic proposal, but it was everything I wanted and so much more. He wanted to surprise me, and that he did!

As the wedding approached, I was flooded with emotions I wasn't exactly ready to deal with. It turned out I hadn't *completely* dealt with my previous divorce as well as I thought I had. I mean how could I have? I was the one who had to be stable and provide for my children. I hadn't had time to have the melt down I so deserved.

It was around Christmas, we were getting married in March. I was beginning to freak out. Is this the right man for me? Are my kids going to like him? Is there someone better out there? Should I just stay single? And then it came, this *big* rush of emotions. All of these feelings I had buried deep down came flooding over. It finally hit me like a brick wall. My last marriage had been a failure, and I had to deal with it. I never regretted my divorce, and I still don't – no doubt about that (cheating rat.) I just think the end of a marriage is like a death. You go into it thinking it is forever with all of these hopes and dreams. It is truly devastating when those dreams come to an end. It is hard to open your heart completely back up and trust again. When you're scared, your mind can entertain all sorts of crazy ideas. What if this marriage fails too? What if I am the problem? What if he cheats on me too? What if things just don't work out? Somebody HELP! I was *trapped.* I couldn't breathe. I couldn't go through with it!

No one gets married and has children without thinking it's forever. Divorce isn't our plan. It's surely not God's plan. So many emotions were sweeping over me all at once. It's then I realized what I needed to find was new hopes and dreams. Life does go on, and it is okay to be happy. God wants us to be happy. Things don't always turn out like we plan, which sometimes is for the best. It's okay for our life plans to change. Often times, our plan is not God's plan. His plan is *so much* better.

If I had it my way, I would have grown up to be a punk rocker (that of course was my childhood dream). I'd be famous by now and on the cover of PEOPLE magazine. Can we say child of the 80's? I mean, I WAS Punky Brewster! I'm not entirely sure what a punk rocker even is, I'm just glad it's not the life I lead. I'm picturing hot pink hair, spiked all over (of course), tights, leg warmers, heels, and definitely a see through shirt sporting a purple bra. Not attractive, no way, God's plan for me was MUCH better.

The time for my wedding had finally arrived! When the big day arrived, I was never more sure of anything in my life. I was marrying the man of my dreams, the man God put here on Earth just for me— my *soul mate*. There were no doubts, no jitters, and no second guesses. He loved me; heck, he was crazy about me! We may have had to travel down narrow roads to find one another, but the point was, we did. I was happier than I had ever been and so were my kids. It's not perfect. We have our fights, tantrums, and melt downs just like everyone else. We make mistakes. We don't always handle things the right way. Unfortunately, there isn't a guide or a book that tells us how to handle everything. I will never forget the feeling of peace and relief I had found at that moment.

It's crazy how wrong we can be at times about our happiness. I truly believed I was happy in my first marriage, and that it was what I wanted.

It never entered my mind there were better options out there for me. It was in that moment I realized I got nothing out of my first marriage. Kevin hadn't cared about my wants or needs. Everything had always been all about him. I had become SO accustomed to just hoping he didn't get drunk, humiliate me at one of the kids' activities, or better yet, catch him cheating on me. I didn't even realize what *happiness* was until I met Derek. I didn't understand what a marriage was and what it should be. It is something sacred and special.

Our wedding was gorgeous and perfect. It was exactly what I had always wanted. We got married in a small chapel with our closest friends and family. I hate being the center of attention or getting up in front of large groups of people, so that made it much easier (the glass of wine I had before may have also helped). After the ceremony, we went to a separate venue where there was a Texas country band, dancing, food, and drinks. We had a blast celebrating us. We danced the night away and enjoyed every moment of it. The kids had a great time too. They had their own little dance party going with all their little friends. That night, they even had a sleep over! What kind of man doesn't mind a sleep over on his wedding night?

Don't get me wrong, I'm not suggesting every person may be happier after their divorce (although I truly think most are), I just know I would not have the happiness I have found today in my first marriage. I truly hate that my children have to deal with the issues that come along with two divorced parents, especially when one is crazy. Hindsight is 20/20. Had I known, I may have made different choices. Had I made different choices, I would not have my three wonderful children. Would I change it for one minute? No, not if it meant not having one of my kids. I'd do it again in a heartbeat; I'd just maybe plan for my divorce a little better from the get go.

For example, I would set up a secret bank account he didn't know about. I would pull out extra cash each time I went to the grocery store and deposit it. I'm just saying, smarter choices. I do think as crazy as my divorce was at times, the stability my kids had in my house only made them better people in the long run. It's better to grow up in a healthy, happy home in my opinion. No one wants that life for their children, but it takes two to make a marriage work. You can't do it alone. We do the best we can and hope we don't screw them up too much in the meantime.

Derek and I went to California for our honeymoon, which was absolutely fantastic. We started with the typical tourist attractions in San Francisco, then traveled our way up to Napa to all of the magnificent wineries. It was beautiful and provided us with ample amount of time to relish in each other and our new marriage. I don't know if I have ever laughed as much as I did throughout the week. It was so nice to have that much time alone with no other distractions – no kids, no games, no fighting, and no bickering back and forth. Leaving Napa, we headed down to Carmel, which was breathtaking. We had rented a convertible sports car and drove the entire way with the top down. The view, the smell of the ocean… it was *breath taking*. The view of the driver in the seat next to me wasn't so bad either, if you know what I'm saying. It was such a relaxing week, which filled us with joy and happiness beyond measure. It was a great start to the lifelong adventure we were beginning together.

## *HAPPILY EVER AFTER*

The honeymoon was over, and we were back to reality (now that took some adjusting). After all, Derek did not have children and was now taking on a 4, 8, and 11-year-old. I am by no means suggesting he was perfect or never lost his cool. It was difficult at times, as I'm sure my children could tell you. The girls were approaching the teenage years and had become accustomed to it just being us. The idea of a man in the house was NOT too appealing to them, as you could imagine. Not to mention, I think I probably catered to them too much and let them get by with plenty of things they shouldn't have after the divorce. I wanted to make up for all the awful things that had happened to them. I wanted things to be as easy for them as possible. This didn't make it any easier for Derek.

Derek had his own idea of how things should be done, and it was a little different than the way it had been. In general, I think while men may be more playful, they are also stricter. This was an adjustment for me as well as the kids. Men have certain *expectations* that are non-negotiable. Women tend to be more understanding. Kids are all different. They respond differently and have different needs.

Looking back, we probably should've read the 5 Love Languages of Parenting ahead of time. This probably would've saved us some major blow-ups. My girls are very different— complete opposites, actually. My oldest daughter was hitting the preteen years—what I like to call the struggle between acting like a child and wanting to be treated like an adult. My second daughter is very much the strong willed middle child. She and Derek had several battles before he FINALLY realized he was better off to pick and choose his battles with her. Although that is something we both struggle with at times! There comes a point at which you realize *nobody* is going to win. My son, the youngest, pretty much bonded with Derek from the get go. He was a momma's boy though, and had pretty much only been around women. I guess you could say he was a little bit sissified, but he was only 4! Derek was determined to turn him into a little boy; he thought we babied him too much. Needless to say, he had his work cut out for him. Now, years later, we laugh and make fun of him. In his defense, I do know it must have been hard— I don't know that I could have done it had roles been reversed. I am so thankful he did not have any children before me! How hypocritical is that? In my opinion he passed with flying colors. He went from single to a ready-made family of 5 overnight. Although rocky at times, we have survived each other thus far. We trudge on; doing the best we can, only growing stronger as a family.

Our bond as a family only grew stronger when we decided to have another child. The kids had mixed emotions, especially my oldest, as she was 13. You can imagine being in junior high and telling your friends your mom is pregnant. By that age, kids pretty much understand the birds and the bees, which means your mom is having S-E-X. Yes, I said it, the dreaded three letter word... S-E-X. Parents are old; we aren't supposed to do that anymore! It was humiliating. I can only imagine the comments she heard at school; I can't really say I blame her.

With time, the kids became excited, yet were still leery of what changes were yet to come until he arrived. Then they were *ecstatic*, constantly fighting over who got to hold him. I think it helped their bond with their stepdad only grow stronger, and I think it helped Derek too. It helped him to know the unconditional love we as parents feel for our children. He always loved my children and was good to them, but now he knew the love I felt for them also, and it changed their relationship for the better. He could understand my views on a different level. He realized why I devoted so much time to them, time that wasn't always available for him.

Life only continued to get better. We added one more child to our family, totaling five, a baby girl. As each year passed, we only became more financially stable. Anyone that knows what it's like to be flat broke, knows what a relief that is. While I believe money can't buy happiness, the lack of it can cause such stress in a relationship.

I remember when I first separated from Kevin, I couldn't even afford to buy groceries. My mom had to drive four and a half hours to Houston just to go to the grocery store. I worked three jobs just to pay the bills, and had to get Derek to pay for Christmas for my kids the first year we were dating. We had many nights of a fun game I liked to call *"let's eat the scraps left in the pantry because we can't afford to make it to the store."* It was such a relief to finally have financial security and not worry about whether or not my debit card would be declined when I was checking out at the grocery store, or worse yet, the dollar store. Things were finally on track, and for the first time in a long time, I was happy and filled with a peace I didn't know existed.

I'm not trying to suggest dating and finding another man to take care of you is the only way to move on. I'm not saying life will be perfect. Some people may not want to hassle with a relationship ever again! Who could blame you? Any relationship is complicated and is going to have its flaws. I think the *key* is finding ourselves. It is SO easy to get wrapped up in being a wife and a mother that we no longer remember who we are or what we want. This is so important as a mom to not only keep our sanity, but to be able to be at our own personal best. We need to be a role model, to teach our kids right from wrong, and to instill the necessary qualities for them to be good, loving, hard working adults.

I know for me, in my first marriage, my life became revolved around my ex-husband and what he wanted, whether or not he was cheating, drunk, or on drugs. I had never really considered what I wanted out of life. What were my goals? What even is happy? I got married and had a child so young I guess I thought that was it. It was whatever my family wanted. I love my kids to the moon and back and would probably have to say they are my hobby, they are my happy, they are *my everything*. The problem is; what do you do when they aren't with you? Who are you going to be when they grow up and leave the house? What do you want the rest of your life to be? What will be your legacy?

For me, I knew I wanted a partner for life, someone I could love and trust. Someone I could depend on to have my back through the stormiest of times. While I was fortunate enough to find it, I also discovered many other things about myself.

I found I needed exercise and time with my girlfriends to unwind. I also love to read, but hadn't taken the time in as long as I could remember. I probably hadn't read a book, at least for enjoyment, since high school. These were all huge stress relievers for me. I also made time to redo things in my house. Pinterest has so many DIY projects that are so rewarding and satisfying— not to mention affordable. I guess you could say, I made more time to focus on me, and things I enjoyed. My kids always have been and always will be my *first* priority, but for the first time in a long time, I was also spending time doing me.

While I feel like I spent time dealing with a divorce and finding myself, along with a new marriage, moving on isn't the hard part—it is *forgiving*. There have been SO many times when I felt happy and at peace, and then the arrogant son of a bitch sends me a nasty message or does something that completely gets under my skin. All of the emotions of anger and hatred toward him I thought I had moved past come flooding back. I honestly can't say if letting go of the anger would be easy or not, if you got along with your ex. I am still, to this day, so filled with anger at times; it's crippling. Truthfully I feel like I may suffer from a little post-traumatic stress disorder from my divorce. I feel a little silly even admitting it. It makes me physically sick at times when I have to deal with him. I don't, however, feel like my anger stems from the past, but more from the present. The past is the reason we got divorced, and I am grateful for it. I am so much better off today than I would've been remaining in that toxic of a marriage. I have so much to be thankful for. He is still to this day so arrogant and selfish, it is hard to swallow at times— especially when he upsets my kids. After everything he has done and put us through, it truly *amazes* me the arrogance and entitlement he still possesses. So, at times, it is hard to move on and let go… especially when you continually have to deal with that person. I think you just have to do the best you can with what you have.

So, that's basically my life story in a nutshell. I screw up daily and have made plenty of mistakes over the years. All we can do is try our best and share what we've learned along the way. Try to focus on the positive in your life and move forward. Truth is, you have to close one door before you can open another.

# WHERE ARE WE NOW

Some people will never change and you just have to accept it. I received a phone call from Jenna, Kevin's first girlfriend shortly after they broke up. When he called things off, he told her it was because she didn't care about his kids (like he cared SO much). She didn't know what he had told the kids and wanted to make sure they knew it wasn't true. He had introduced the new girlfriend to them before he ever called things off with Jenna. During their time together, he cheated on her multiple times, and she even caught him trying to get a prostitute once right after they had gotten back from a trip. They weren't having issues.

In that moment, she realized Kevin doing that to me had nothing to do with our relationship. I guess it's just easier to believe someone is just unhappy when they cheat, rather than accepting it is just who they are. We might have to admit to ourselves they would do it to us. Even though

Jenna's own mother used to tell her, "*Take a good look at his ex-wife because that will be you,*" she couldn't do it. She stayed anyway. She said she always took my side in fights because he never put the kids first; yet, she still stayed. Why do we as women stay? Why do we want to fix people? Why is it always easier to believe the ex is just a terrible person, but we are different? He won't do those things to you; you are special. Please, ladies. Open your eyes.

Kevin went through several moves (and women) and ended up 15 miles away from us. Over time, he has gotten significantly easier to deal with in comparison to the first few years (props to the new wife); believe me when everyone tells you the first year is the worst... it's true.

While things were better, we still were having our fair share of heated arguments until one weekend—everything came to a head. My daughter had a basketball tournament; in between games, he wanted her to drive 30 minutes back to his house to attend church. She did not want to go with him and refused to get in the car. Immediately the messages started, like I had any control over the situation. I told her to go with him for Pete's sake! Things escalated to a new level, and my husband got involved.

Derek stayed out of the drama between Kevin and I for a long period of time. We always thought him becoming involved would make it worse. Derek had enough, and after arguing back and for with Kevin, he messaged Kevin's wife. She was obviously upset by these messages (which were nothing compared to the abusive crap Kevin had been sending for years). Kevin accused Derek of bullying his wife. So, Derek told him, *"From now on, every time you send my wife ugly messages, I will send your wife ugly messages and we'll see how she likes it."* I have not gotten an ugly message since.

Kevin remarried a couple years after me, in fact he just had his 2nd child with his new wife— she has lasted much longer than I thought she would. I would imagine two children under the age of two has been quite eye opening. Prior to the delivery of their first child, we had a final blow up. They had moved about 15 miles away from us, and did not tell us they were moving for whatever reason. This was the last ugly message I received. My son had a baseball game and I hadn't told them about it (side note: it was posted online and they had internet access). Mind you, it was not their weekend, and I didn't even know they were moving. This was my response to his message, some are responses to other crazy accusations he had about summer visitation, vacation, etc. This is how you do it ladies. Put it in writing, leave no margin for error, and document everything. This was the last *personal* attack (Disclaimer: they also had their first baby shortly after, I'm sure it helped).

1. Let it be known that I didn't have to correct the dates you gave me. That was me, being nice. I won't bother in the future.

2. Let it be known I sent our vacation because we are going with my entire family

that week regardless of your schedule. If notification 3 months ahead of time is not enough notice and you need to go that week, feel free. The kids just won't go with us.

3. I'm not your personal secretary. I'm actually not required to notify you of any events. You have access to the same websites I do. Me notifying you in the past is me being nice.

4. I'm not a psychic. I don't know your work schedule or when y'all are or aren't available, nor do I care. I must've missed the email where you asked if anyone had anything this weekend, week, or month.

5. If you were free this weekend, an appropriate response would be....surprise! We moved to Granville! Does anyone have anything this weekend? By the way, Paisley had a basketball tournament. The link to her schedule was sent to you months ago. The link to Conner's baseball has been sent to y'all for the past several years. I didn't realize I needed to resend it every season.

6. Please stop victimizing yourselves that y'all are mistreated and never told anything. You have access to every website. Every kid has a cell phone. I am available by phone or email to also inquire about their activities. I must've missed all the phone calls, texts, or emails y'all have sent asking about them.

7. If I wanted to be "rude" I would point out that you get the kids for no more than 2 periods of at least 7 days totaling no more than 30. Once again I was being nice and trying to work with you

8. Please stop pretending y'all are "reaching out" by sending your snide messages when you turn around and get ugly less than 24 hrs. later. I was simply explaining I didn't even know y'all moved until Sat evening. I'm not sure what I was supposed to respond to Erin's message. I sent her the information she asked for. But hey you had 7 days to notify me, I'll be more than happy to treat y'all with the same respect y'all have always given me.

9. If y'all really want to get along and work together, this is not the way to go about it. Then again you've never grasped that concept. Your messages are condescending and y'all are complete hypocrites.

It has been almost 10 years since my divorce was final. We have survived. Things, for the most part, are better. We can now communicate by text. We still don't speak in person or act like we know each other, but I am working on that. We are and always will be a work in progress. It has been over a year since our last big fight. So far, the kids have all turned out somewhat normal and successful—although, we are all a *little crazy* in our own way. My daughters are now 16 and 19; my son is almost 12.

My girls don't have much of a relationship with their father; nor, anyone else in his family for that matter. No one ever put forth too much effort. Kevin and his family put forth more focus on trying to make them out to be terrible, spoiled, ungrateful, bratty kids. This only made them resent his family and never want much to do with them. Kids are the best judges of character after all. I guess it was supposed to be reflective of my parenting? Can we say backfire? Needless to say, it didn't hurt me; it hurt their own relationship with the kids. My advice to the family of a divorced couple— the only side you should choose is that of the kids. They are the number one priority. Not your son or daughter. If everyone is looking at the kids' best interest, getting along should be easy.

Kevin's behavior is still *erratic* at times, although there has been a BIG improvement. He does make somewhat of an effort, with my son and occasionally kind of tries with my daughters (because his wife requires it). I'm not sure if it's a blessing or a curse. She seems nice enough, just young and naïve. It is really not her fault she lacks the life experience to know the things he says are bullshit. After all, it took me 10 years. She was super gung ho in the beginning—bound and determined to fix everything for him…because then their relationship would have been fixed, right? She too will figure it out, and I kind of think she has started to get it. I truly hope I am wrong, but I know what is in her future, and one day she will too. He continues to practice medicine and for all I know has never been caught abusing drugs or alcohol on the job. Oh wait, he's been "*clean*" since we got divorced. He did it ALL by himself, who needs rehab anyway? Hallelujah! (Please note the sarcasm).

Not much else has changed from my perspective; although in some ways, everything has changed. Kevin still does nothing wrong. In fact, my girls constantly wrong him. It must be hard to always be the victim. He half ass attends some of their activities, he comes to the bare minimum, he doesn't get them extra time, he does nothing extra at all, and he is still just as selfish as he ever was. His lack of involvement and effort has been a blessing for me. On a positive note there are no threats, ugly messages, name calling, or unnecessary added stress. There is no more fighting, and we pretty much stick to the divorce decree only. That's the point things came to. I could no longer work with him at all and had to go solely by the decree after our last big blow up.

I used to let Kevin pick his weekends because of his work schedule. He would never give us notice, wanted to change everything at the last minute (regardless of what the kids had planned), and his fits were unbearable. His tantrums were worse than that of a toddler. It was more than we could all take. I guess that is what the decree is for, to eliminate disagreements for those of us who can't act like adults. That was the best decision I made, and I wish I had done it sooner. I always thought it would make it worse for me and the kids; but in fact, it was liberating. It gave us a schedule to follow and the ability to make plans that could not be changed unless we wanted them changed. It gave us *control* of our own lives, something we had not had in years.

My oldest daughter Brittany now attends the University of Texas. She had a 4.0 this year, she graduated 3rd in her class, was a cheerleader, went to state in academic UIL multiple times, played volleyball and golf, and worked part time as a waitress her last year of high school. She is an amazing young lady. Driven, motivated, kind, and caring. She continues to occasionally speak to her dad every couple months and is always willing to give him another chance, no matter how many times he lets her down. Through all the fights and disappointments, he is still her father. I think she must partly remember the father from when she was young. The man that was kind, caring, and loving. Maybe that's just her heart. Christ teaches us to love as He loves us. Her dad does not help pay for college. He has not done so much as send her $20. He has not called her once, nor has he ever gone to see her or where she lives. He did tell her this past Christmas that he has finally figured out his starting point in helping. He will pay for her books, after she buys them and provides him with a receipt. She is responsible, and has never given anyone a reason not to trust her. I think you can imagine what she told him at that point. He then proceeded to tell her she was dramatic and that sometimes you have to be the bigger person and make all the effort. You see, it was her fault all along they never had a relationship! Not his. Apparently, he is not a parent or an adult, and there lies the problem. My husband and I have paid close to $30,000 for her education thus far. You can keep your $200, dick. We got this. She still desires a relationship with her dad. That's okay. It's her decision and it has to be her decision when she is done trying. Regardless, she has turned out to be an amazing daughter and we could not be more proud.

Paisley is a sophomore in high school. Kevin has attended two of her basketball games (she plays two nights a week). I don't know when she saw him last. She makes straight A's, and like her sister, is driven, motivated, and a strong person. She sees her father for who he is; only she is not easily manipulated, like her sister Brittany. She most often does not respond to his messages, and

I can't say I blame her. She is the typical middle child. She can be stubborn and hard to deal with at times. The more you try to force something on her, the more she will resist. She has been this way since the beginning. He has basically given up with her. While I know it's sad, I think she is better off without him. She has plenty of positive male role models in her life. She is strong and beautiful; she will be fine. Not too long ago, he had been texting and calling her. She would not respond or answer. He texted me and asked me to have her call him. I pleaded with her to just call, talk for a couple minutes; this would fulfill whatever it was in him driving the phone calls, and then she would probably hear nothing from him for months. Her words... *"He's weird, I don't even know him and I don't want to talk to him. He never talks to me; why do I have to talk to him now?"* I get it. It is weird. She was only 6 when we divorced and does not have a memory of a dad that was ever there for her. She remembers that he got her and wouldn't feed her, made her pick up trash on the side of the road, made her miss her games and her friends' sleepovers. He was never there to dry the tears, help her with homework, or watch her score the winning basket. He has never called her to check on her and ask how she is. He never tried to be a part of her life; he only forced her to be part of his when it was convenient for him. She is not her sister. She is wired differently, and it's all just weird to her. That's okay. It's her decision; after all, I think she is old enough to choose who she wants in her life.

Conner is a loving boy. He is almost 12 and is a pleaser. He gets along with everyone. He still goes to see his dad. If his dad doesn't get him, he is every bit as happy to stay home. He is easy. His dad has used his kindness and eagerness to please against his sisters on more than one occasion, which has been really disappointing for me. The last thing I would ever do as a parent is try to turn my kids against each other. Obviously, if Kevin can get along with the son, it is the girl's fault he can't get along with them.

Conner is a great kid. He does not even remember his dad or me ever being married. When he sees old pictures, he thinks it is weird to even see us together. It's hilarious, really. It just goes to show you if you keep the kids out of it and they are young, it doesn't really affect them. He was only two when we divorced. He has no memory of the crazy things his dad did during the first couple years of our divorce. If his dad does not come to his games, he assumes he's working or busy and does not think twice about it. He has no expectations of his dad, really. Kevin usually comes to Conner's activities if it is his weekend, but other than that, he doesn't come too much. For Kevin to do anything extra— Conner would never expect it.

Derek tries to stay out of everything for the most part. We try to keep the focus on our family and our lives. Kevin is not part of it, nor does he deserve to bc. Derek was recently doing some work for a local homebuilder, and when the owners were brought over for the final walk through, it was Kevin and his wife. They spoke for the very first time— mind you, we have been married almost 7 years.

It turned into about an hour-long conversation of Derek telling Kevin how great and responsible his kids are. He thought he really got somewhere, and afterward, nothing changed (surprise, surprise). The funny part about it was during that time, Kevin started paying me large sums of child support, $15,000, to be exact. You see, he never notified the attorney general's office when he changed jobs. They would have to track him down and get everything set up, so months would go by without us receiving any child support. In Texas, you can't close on a house if you have child support in arrears. That's karma, people. He may not pay half of their medical bills like he is supposed to, but he didn't get by with that one! It's what I call *winning*!

Derek is an awesome husband and stepfather to my children. I really lucked out when God gave him to me. He is a loving father and husband, a great provider, and most importantly, he is honest. There is nothing more important in a relationship than trust. Derek is successful and has built his own company from the ground up, which allows him the flexibility to be home every evening and make it to most of the kids' activities. Although we would be fine without the child support, that's not the point. The point is, they are Kevin's kids, and legally, he has to help support them—otherwise Kevin can sign them over to Derek, and he will gladly pay for everything. If we are going to have to share holidays, weekends, and summers, he can pay what he is legally obligated too. Derek loves and supports us all, without resentment or strings attached. He did not have any children before he met me, and I know it was a huge commitment.

I had always wanted to go to graduate school and finish with my nurse practitioner. I had been an RN for over 10 years. It had always been something I wanted, but put on hold for my family. After all, my ex-husband was in medical school and I had kids, someone had to work and take care of them. Why we as women are notorious for being the ones to volunteer for that, I will never understand. I guess it's maternal instinct. So that's what I did. I worked and took care of my children. Raising kids is THE most important job there is. I am now proud to say I am also a Family Nurse Practitioner. It had always been a dream of mine, and I finally achieved it.

Completing my degree has been SO fulfilling and satisfying, I can't even begin to explain it. Furthering my education has empowered me and allowed me to gain a new confidence I hadn't felt before. I am so lucky to have such a supportive husband and family that want to see me succeed. I had two kids with Derek while in graduate school, leaving me with a total of 5. I never took a semester off during my pregnancies, either. I knew I had to keep going. I had to finish. Determined, I just took it slow, and went part time. Graduating feels like I am at the *top of my mountain.* Life was such a struggle for so long. I've finally reached that turning point. I have a great career, I have great patients, an amazing husband, 5 healthy, spectacular children, and I have been blessed beyond measure. Every rock, stump, bump, or log in the road was worth it. I didn't let life beat me. With God's help I won, and it is only going to get better from here.

# IT IS WHAT IT IS

It isn't always about who's right and who's wrong. The bottom line is sometimes in life, we are never going to get the apology we feel we are owed or the recognition we deserve. The longer we hang on waiting for it, the further we are from reaching our goal. We have to take whatever steps are necessary to achieve closure. We have to let go and accept things for what they are. That was (and is) one of the hardest parts for me.

I had been hurt and seriously wronged. Worst of all, I knew I had done nothing to deserve it. It's not about who deserves what though. It took me a long time to realize that. That's not how life works. The fact of the matter is, I was a damn good wife and mother. I knew it, and deep down, Kevin knew it too. Was I perfect? Of course not, but who is? I had given 110% to my marriage and didn't deserve what I got. Plain and simple— and that is something that will never be acknowledged. And it is okay. I know the truth, and God knows the truth. What else really matters anyway?

To my ex and his family, I will always be the *evil* ex-wife who took his kids from him and ruined his life. That, for me, was one of the hardest parts to swallow, especially after all he had put us through. In my mind, I had no other options, other than to stay and be a doormat. I had to do what was best for me and my children. If they need to believe it was my fault, so be it. He was a master manipulator, after all, who knows what they were told. I was never going to get a sincere apology, acknowledgement of any of his wrong doings, nothing. I was never going to get the recognition and respect I deserved for raising his children. Instead, I got just the opposite. Any chance he had to *criticize* my parenting, or even worse, my children, he was going to capitalize on. Eventually you come to the realization that what matters is how your kids see you, not your EX in laws, friends, etc.

It's true though, keep your mouth shut, and they will reap what they sow. The worse he tried to make me look, the worse he looked. Here he was, trying to play the poor, single dad card. Really, asshole? You get your kids maybe one weekend a month, you don't call them, you don't come watch their activities, you don't have a relationship with them; yet, you want to criticize the one person who has always been there for them? Believe me, that has never taken him very far with them and never will. Of course that's not what I want for my kids. They don't deserve that. Nothing has made them angrier over the years. I am their *person*, it is an insult to them as much as it is to me.

Ideally, in a perfect world, Kevin and I would get along and raise our kids together, as friends, even. We can all dream, but that doesn't make it a reality. When you've been dealing with the arrogant sack of shit I've been dealing with for the past 10 years, however, it does give you peace of mind to know truth prevails. I can sit back, focus on the positives in my life, and my kids see through him. I don't have to be negative. I don't have to try and make him look bad or compete with him and the new wife or girlfriend, bless her heart. I am their mother and I always will be. That is my only focus and concern. That's all that matters. He missed out on all of the little moments…first dances, first kisses, first boyfriends, first break ups. He lost. He spent so much time trying to get even he lost sight of what really mattered.

I guess that's how I finally found my closure. I can remember him wanting to meet a year after we got divorced. He gave me some *half-ass* apology and wanted my advice on fixing his relationship with his kids. What a joke? That would involve him taking some responsibility and changing who he was, which would never happen. I played along, however, and gave him my two cents. I told him I could care less he had cheated, after all, that's why we were divorced, but I did have a huge problem with what an ass he had been to deal with ever since. Once again, he gave a half-ass apology. Did anything change? Hell no. He left, took my kids and made them pick up trash on the side of the road for probably an hour, without lunch (mind you this was during the first year of our divorce). What a *peach* of a dad he was. As usual, he listened to nothing I said. He had no real interest in hearing anything I had to say or fixing his relationship with his children. It was obvious the meeting was a result of his girlfriend's bright idea, or he was faking the next step in his AA recovery. Regardless, I have no doubt that in his mind it was, how did the new wife put it, teaching them responsibility and they believe in *"eating healthy."* He has a knack for twisting truths. He is so convincing, I think he even convinces himself.

Well here is a piece of my favorite advice: A little girl seeks revenge. A real woman moves on while karma does her dirty work. Point being, you don't have to compete. You don't have to argue or even win the argument. In the end, things will turn out the way they are meant to. We don't have to get even or seek revenge. We just have to move forward. We have to learn to *accept* things for what they are. There are some things in this life we will never be able to control.

It took me a long time to realize it wasn't always personal. He truly suffers from mental illness, and sadly, he can't always control it. It's his way or no way. When it doesn't happen, he lashes out; it's like a reflex. He's not trying to get even or make my life difficult. It's all about him and how it is affecting him. He will always have these ups and downs. He will go from one extreme to the next. We will hear from him consistently for a while, and then we won't. It's the nature of the beast. Once I finally understood, it made it so much easier to move forward and accept things for what they were. He is classic Bipolar at the very least. The sex, drugs, drinking. It all FINALLY made sense.

I guess for some people maybe a letter, a conversation, or possibly counseling can help achieve the closure they need. For sure it might help you to understand a little sooner than I did. For me, I spent time in prayer and talking to friends and family. I did talk some with my pastor's wife in Kingwood, and my pastor once I moved. In the end, I had to let go. I was never going to get what I thought I was owed or deserved. Truth was, no matter what I did he and his family would always treat me as negative. After all, that was the only way they could live with all he had done—by blaming me for everything possible. I could live with that. After all, it's not a lot to live with.

You can always tell how miserable people are with their own life— when they're always looking for ways to destroy someone else's. I would always be the big, evil bitch. Everything would always be my fault... even their lack of relationship with my children. They would never make an effort; it would be so much easier to just play the martyr.  Once I came to that realization and quit trying, things got better.  I moved forward.  As the saying goes, let go and let God.  That's exactly what I did.  It's not always easy, as I still have to deal with him, but time really does heal all.  Things are SO much better than they used to be.  There are times I still get angry, don't get me wrong, I am by no means perfect.  There are times you need to do as I say and not as I do.  I just have to remember there is only so much I can control (thank goodness for the divorce decree, guidelines are key).  Anything beyond that I have to let go, I can't change things; they are what they are.  This is my life and the hand I have been dealt, and all I can do is make the best of it.

Closure isn't about getting the apology you deserved or hearing that person admit the truth of what they did wrong.  It really doesn't even involve anyone else.  It's about finding peace with a situation and moving forward.  It's about *taking* whatever steps are necessary in order to find your own peace. Accepting your situation for what it is and *realizing* it's up to you to find your own happiness. Don't let anyone else take it away from you. Closure is a choice, not something that just happens. We have one life. We should live it to its fullest capacity and never settle for anything less. Forge ahead, make your own life and let nothing stand in your way. Your life is about YOU. *The past cannot be changed, forgotten, edited, or erased; it can only be ACCEPTED.* – *Author unknown*

Made in the USA
San Bernardino, CA
25 July 2018